Fifty Years of *Studies in Intelligence*

Nicholas Dujmovic

> **Looking back upon the more than 1,200 articles in *Studies*, we see that Sherman Kent indeed established something enduring.**

A half-century has passed since Sherman Kent lamented the lack of an "intelligence literature" and decided to do something about it—a bold step, even for as nimble a bureaucracy as the CIA was alleged to be. Today, looking back upon the more than 1,200 article-length contributions that comprise five decades of *Studies in Intelligence*, we see that Kent indeed established something enduring. Somewhere along the way, *Studies* went from being Kent's revolutionary idea to becoming an institution. And yet, *Studies* continues to be revolutionary in its insistence on remaining an unofficial publication for the best thinking on intelligence from the entire profession—thinking that is often provocative, always cogent, and inevitably adds to the corpus of intelligence literature.

This reflection on the past 50 years of *Studies in Intelligence* is based on my experience as a long-time reader, a sometime contributor, and a current member of its editorial board. In addition, I spent much of the summer of 2005 going through all the issues of *Studies* since it appeared in 1955—a fascinating journey in itself. In keeping with a tradition unbroken since the first issue, the thoughts expressed here are my own, reflect no official views whatsoever, and are intended as much to provoke discussion as to

inform. I have also decided to include interesting or odd facts that my research has uncovered, for the benefit of the true *Studies* junkies I know are out there.

Humble Beginnings

Even if one knew that Sherman Kent during 1953–54 had argued for the creation of a scholarly publication on intelligence (along with an Institute for the Advanced Study of Intelligence), it would be a mistake to say that what Kent first begot was an actual journal.[1] It was really an experiment to test the viability of a journal.

The small-format, yellow, soft-cover publication that emerged

Nicholas Dujmovic serves on the CIA History Staff.

> ## 66
> ## The modest publication that emerged in 1955 had none of the hallmarks of a journal.
> ## 99

from the CIA's Office of Training in September 1955 was a modest endeavor with none of the hallmarks of a journal: no declaration that this was "volume one, number one," no masthead, no editors listed by name, and no self-description as a journal.[2] Calling itself a "monograph series," the first *Studies* led with Kent's famous essay, still worth reading, on the need for the intelligence discipline to have a literature that would result in the accumulation of knowledge necessary to form the basis of a true profession. The second half of

---

[1] Harold P. Ford, "A Tribute to Sherman Kent," *Studies in Intelligence* 24, no. 3 (1980). Kent's idea for an institute was not realized until 1974, with the creation of the Center for the Study of Intelligence, which became the home for the journal.
[2] The 5½-by-8¾–inch format lasted through 1972.

In May 1956, *Studies* focused on economic intelligence.

that first issue comprised the unnamed editors' thoughts on how Kent's proposal should be accomplished, namely, that the publication should be unofficial, contain a mix of classified and unclassified articles, avoid publishing anything resembling a finished intelligence product, and put forward the "best views" of CIA people—there was as yet little thought given to the Intelligence Community, which in the mid-1950s existed more in theory than in practice. Responsible debate would be encouraged and the submissions were not to be "coordinated" in order to let "experienced officers systematically speak their minds"—all with the goal of supporting the development of intelligence into a "respected profession."[3]

The next two issues emerged roughly on a quarterly basis and continued in the same "monograph series" vein: the January

---

[3] Sherman Kent, "The Need for an Intelligence Literature," *Studies in Intelligence* [hereafter *Studies*], September 1955. In the same issue, "The Editors" contributed their ideas on "The Current Program for an Intelligence Literature." *Studies'* archives indicate that Charles M. Lichenstein wrote the essay. Editor Lichenstein would later become the deputy US representative to the United Nations who in 1983 famously invited the UN to depart the United States ("We will put no impediment in your way and we will be at the dockside bidding you a farewell as you set off into the sunset").

1956 issue, with two articles on assessing capabilities, and the May issue, with two on economic intelligence. The authorship was impressive and was no doubt meant to be: Abbot Smith of the Board of National Estimates wrote one of the articles; Max Millikan, of the Massachusetts Institute of Technology, who had helped create economic intelligence at the CIA, wrote another.[4] Two soon-to-be-standard features appeared at this early date: a "bibliographic section" that would evolve into *Studies'* popular book review section, and informed commentary on articles recently published. The foundation of an "intelligence litera-

---

[4] Abbot Smith, "Notes on Capabilities in National Intelligence," *Studies*, January 1956. Max Millikan, "The Nature and Methods of Economic Intelligence," *Studies*, May 1956.

Studies 1, no. 4, 1957, the first numbered issue.

ture"—as well as necessary discussion about it—had begun.

Studies Breaks Out as a Journal

Even with this impressive start and the backing of senior CIA leaders, there was an interval of some 16 months before *Studies in Intelligence* burst forth as a journal in the fall of 1957 with volume 1, number 4. While the record is silent on the reason for the delay, it is reasonable to speculate that Kent wanted that issue to make a splash. Consequently, the first issue of *Studies* as a bona fide journal contained nine articles (by such luminaries as Ray Cline, R. J. Smith, Ed Allen, and Air Force intelligence chief John Samford), three book reviews, and some recommendations by Walter Pforzheimer on further reading. Topics included the relationship of intelligence to strategy, the coordination process (an eternal bugaboo!), technical collection, how to approach research, and industrial intelligence. This early *Studies* was primarily, but not exclusively, a CIA venture: The lead article by Gen. Samford, as well as the editors' appeal for articles "from any member of the Intelligence Community," represented an understanding that the "literature of intelligence" should not be a CIA monopoly. To show the highest level support for the new venture, Director of Central Intelligence (DCI) Allen Dulles provided a foreword that noted its value "as a dynamic means of refining our doctrines . . . [that]

> ## " The early *Studies* was primarily, but not exclusively, a CIA venture. "

cannot but improve our capabilities to turn out a better product."[5]

Sporting a new cover and a masthead that included the listing of a distinguished editorial board headed by Sherman Kent, the first issue as a journal also put forward the journal's editorial policy. Undoubtedly written by Kent himself, that policy has continued without substantive change to this day:

• *Articles for the* Studies in Intelligence *may be written on any theoretical, doctrinal, operational, or historical aspect of intelligence.*[6]

• *The final responsibility for accepting or rejecting an article rests with the Editorial Board.*

• *The criterion for publication is whether or not, in the opinion of the Board, the article makes a*

---

[5] It was not clear early on whether the *Studies* was [were?] a singular or a plural. In the Fall 1957 issue, for example, DCI Dulles remarks that "the *Studies* are designed to bridge the gap between experience and inexperience" and yet commends "the *Studies in Intelligence* to you and wish it all success in its mission" (author's emphasis).

[6] Yes, "the" *Studies in Intelligence*. Perhaps because of the journal's start as "the *Studies* [monograph] series," the definite article was attached and would live on in the journal's editorial policy statement until 1994.

contribution to the literature of intelligence.

Besides setting forth an enduring editorial policy, the issue also established the editorial board as the last word on what appeared in *Studies*. The first board included probably as formidable a group of CIA minds as could be assembled: Sherman Kent, then head of the Board of National Estimates, as chairman; Inspector General Lyman Kirkpatrick; General Counsel Lawrence Houston; senior economist Edward Allen; and former Legislative Counsel Walter Pforzheimer.

The Sherman Kent Legacy

The success of *Studies* that we are commemorating in this jubilee year owes much to Sherman Kent, who not only conceived and nurtured the idea of a professional intelligence journal, but also continued to oversee its development until his retirement in 1968.

Kent sought the widest possible distribution for *Studies*. Recognizing the challenges, he warned in

Sherman Kent

Book Reviews in *Studies*:
Intelligent Literature about Intelligence Literature

Judging both from readers' comments over the years and from the enthusiasm demonstrated in the contributions received, the book review section of *Studies in Intelligence* has long been a favorite—for many, *the* favorite—part of the journal. Sherman Kent's initial essay did not explicitly cite the need for book reviews, but the September 1955 issue included a promise from the editors for a section reviewing the "literature which can sometimes be studied with profit by intelligence officers." Indeed, the second issue premiered such a "Bibliographic Section," intended to highlight "books or articles . . . that have a close relation to the subject of a [*Studies* article] . . . . This will have the primary purpose of directing the reader's attention to items in the existing literature, overt and classified, which in our judgment make a contribution to the development of sound intelligence doctrine." Kent himself wrote the first review (anonymously) and, according to *Studies'* archives, eventually wrote eight more.

Studies quickly abandoned the idea of reviewing books connected solely to the subject matter in its articles: The first issue of *Studies* as a journal (Fall 1957) contained three classified critiques of current books that had little to do with the articles, plus it debuted Walter Pforzheimer's compendium of mini-reviews of intelligence-related books that the editors "thought looked interesting enough to call to the attention of the readers of these *Studies in Intelligence*." Herewith was set a structure and pattern that exists to this day. The mini-review subsection has gone by various names over the years—"We Spied . . . ," "Public Texts in Intelligence," "Briefly Noted," "Books in Brief," and "The Intelligence Officer's Bookshelf"—but the overall book review section has been titled "Intelligence in Recent Public Literature" since late 1959—another enduring (and perhaps endearing) *Studies* tradition.

The value of a book review in *Studies*, as readers long ago figured out, related to the special knowledge, experience, or position of the reviewer. Who would not find irresistible, for example, a review of Christopher Andrew's *For the President's Eyes Only*, by longtime PDB editor and White House briefer Chuck Peters? Or Dick Holms's review of a book on the war in Laos? Whether it was Sherman Kent on an OSS history, Walter Pforzheimer on a biography of Allen Dulles, Frank Wisner on Dulles's *Craft of Intelligence*, or George Allen on a treatment of Vietnam, readers could rely on *Studies* to provide assessments of intelligence literature unavailable anywhere else. Reviews, of course, often reveal something about the reviewer: It is possible still to marvel at William Colby's review of a book on World War II operations in Norway—where he had operated while in the OSS—in which he not once uses the personal pronoun "I."

Readers also could count on frank language, particularly for those books to be avoided. One wonders whether word ever got back to L. Fletcher Prouty about what Walter Pforzheimer thought of his book about the CIA, *The Secret Team:* "Reading it is like trying to push a penny with one's nose through molten fudge." Christine Flowers, who did the mini-review section for several years, was a master of the withering one-liner: "A vicious little book by a vile little man" (Joseph B. Smith's *Portrait of a Cold Warrior*) and "A second-rate book about a second-rate operation bungled by second-rate officers" (Henry Hurt, *Shadrin*) are two of her best.

Occasionally, *Studies* would single out a significant book for extraordinary treatment. One such case was Thomas Powers's *The Man Who Kept the Secrets*, which was discussed at length in a review essay by John Bross in the Spring 1980 issue, accompanied by shorter reviews by Walter Pforzheimer and Donald Gregg, each bringing a different perspective. Whether one agrees with reviews or not, they always make for great reading.

> ## " Many of the early articles still stand up after decades. "

the initial issue that "the plain fact is that 'security' [note the word's placement in quotation marks] and the advance of knowledge are in fundamental conflict." He got his way, at least for the first few issues. Beginning in 1959, however, the requests for foreign dissemination and release to foreign nationals required the existence of *Studies* to "be treated as information privy to the US official community." Moreover, issues from 1964 on were numbered and subject to recall. The warning about the journal's existence and the numbering of issues were dropped in 1992. Not only was *Studies* preparing its first all-unclassified

---

The *Studies in Intelligence* Editorial Board

Over the years, the *Studies* editorial board has comprised a virtual *Who's Who* drawn from all directorates of the CIA and, increasingly, the Intelligence Community. More than 100 individuals have served on the board. The longest serving was Laurence Houston, at 19 years. Four current members have served for more than 10 years each: William Nolte (13), Jon Wiant (13), Dawn Eilenberger (11), and Denis Clift (10).

In line with its charter, the board, at its quarterly meetings, discusses all submissions presented to it by the editor, who has the authority to cull indisputably below-standard items. Board members read and prepare commentary on several dozen articles on average. They all have demanding jobs; devoting time to this kind of careful and thoughtful review is a tribute to their commitment to the quality of *Studies in Intelligence*.

---

issue that year, but also maintaining secrecy about the journal's existence seemed silly in the wake of the "coming out" of both the *President's Daily Brief* and the National Reconnaissance Office.

From the beginning, it was recognized that unclassified articles and reviews were valuable and should be handled differently. Starting with the Spring 1958 issue, the journal was published in two sections. The unclassified section, often with two or three articles and book reviews, had its own table of contents and was intended to be separated from the main issue. This practice was discontinued after Kent's retirement, and unclassified articles were merely marked as such within the classified issues. The first wholly unclassified issue appeared in 1992, a reprint of selected items from previous issues. Today, half the issues each year are unclassified and readers know that the green-covered *Studies* can be taken home, while the blue-covered ones must stay at the office. Kent would be pleased by the wide distribution *Studies* now receives through its electronic posting on classified and unclassified Web sites.[7]

Under Kent's direction, *Studies* quickly established itself as a well-written, provocative, and

---

[7] Internet site: http://www.cia.gov/csi/studies.html.

---

eclectic publication of intelligence theory and practice, with articles of high quality and relevance, many of which still stand up after decades. In the Summer 1958 issue, for example, the experience of various interrogation experts was brought together for an article that might profitably be read today by counterterrorism officers. Those considering working in the Mideast today would benefit from the cross-cultural advice for operations officers provided in 1964 with "Face Among the Arabs." Ray Cline's 1957 piece, "Is Intelligence Over-Coordinated?" (answer: yes), would provide perspective to those grappling today with the issue. Present-day analysts can take heart from Frank Knapp's observation in the Spring 1964 issue that editors change analysts' drafts in mystifying ways. Students of intelligence failure should study Sherman Kent's own mea culpa regarding his mistaken view in September 1962 that the Soviets would not risk placing offensive missiles in Cuba.[8]

A selection from the articles mentioned above illustrates that the high quality articles were also eminently readable:

---

[8] Peter Naffsinger, "Face Among the Arabs," *Studies* 8, no. 3 (Summer 1964); Ray Cline, "Is Intelligence Over-Coordinated?" *Studies* 1, no. 4 (Fall 1957); Frank Knapp, "Styles and Stereotypes in Intelligence Studies," *Studies* 8, no. 2 (Spring 1964); Sherman Kent, "A Crucial Estimate Relived," *Studies* 8, no. 2 (Spring 1964).

Mystery Writers

Have you ever looked over the table of contents of an issue of *Studies*, or its list of contributors, and wondered "Why haven't I heard of this or that person?" Over the years, but particularly in its first two decades, many contributors to *Studies* chose to conceal their true identities with pen names. Overall, more than 15 percent of the articles written for *Studies* have appeared under false names.

As for the pen names themselves, some in their Anglo-Saxonness have been quite ordinary, probably deliberately so: "Martha Anderson" and "Richard Framingham," for example. Others, no doubt inside jokes, sound positively Monty Pythonesque ("Thomas Meeksbroth," "R. H. Sheepshanks"). Several were more appropriate for romance novels ("Horatio Aragon," "Adam Jourdonnais," "Carlos Revilla Arango") but admittedly were improvements on the true names. And a few were real hoots: The author of an article on the importance of learning foreign languages was "Pierre Ali Gonzales-Schmidt," and a critique of an article was submitted by "Ralph Riposte." Then we have the single word monikers: "Inquirer," "Expatriate," "Onlooker," "Diogenes," and "Chronomaniac" (who wrote a piece on geo-time and intelligence).

Some pseudonymous authors apparently sought transformation. Writing on Chinese factories, one writer Sinocized himself. Another with a stout Irish name became "Viktor Kamenev"—this for an article on "The Standardization of Foreign Personal Names." A senior officer with an easy Italian name became "J. J. Charlevois," when he was not "A. V. Knobelspiesse." Several male authors used female pseudonyms; one received three *Studies* awards as "Rita." By contrast, in 50 years there was only one case in which a female writer sought anonymity as a male.

The collective imperative would sometimes be manifest: Coauthors would use one pen name—in one case, four authors with perfectly fine names combined under "Max Hatzenbeuhler" to write about operations in a certain region. One of the journal's most prolific authors wrote under a different nom de plume no less than 13 times, using such diverse monikers as "Anthony Quibble," "Don Compos," "Sandra Richcreek," and "Eduardo Tudelo." He wrote under his own name, too, and in keeping with the sanctity of *Studies'* pen names, I will not disclose it here. By contrast, many names sounded like pseudonyms but were not. I was wrongly convinced that Ernest Chase, for example, must have been a counterintelligence officer (he was an economist at the State Department).

While it is not surprising that CIA operations officers wrote for *Studies* under cover—tradecraft habits die hard—until now it was not widely known that some famous ones had been *Studies* authors: Eloise Page, Cord Meyer, Ray Rocca, Ray Garthoff, Peter Bagley, Theodore Shackley, Frederic Schultheis, and Joe Hayes. Readers will have to guess which articles they wrote.

Finally, there are those pseudonymous authors of *Studies* who are TNU—True Name Unknown. They submitted their drafts anonymously, with a pen name attached, and their identities simply were never recorded by the *Studies* staff. If someone knows the true identities of the following, please let me know: "Lester Hajek," "Charles Marvel," "Albert Riffice," "Gabriel D'Echauffour."

> ## " At the helm of *Studies*, Sherman Kent particularly nurtured comprehensiveness and eclecticism. "

- Interrogation experts: *Maltreating the subject is from a strictly practical point of view as short-sighted as whipping a horse to his knees before a thirty-mile ride.*

- Cline: *Being in favor of coordination in the US intelligence community has come to be like being against sin; everyone lines up on the right side of the question.*

- Knapp: *The editor smoothes the ruffled feelings of the analyst in the following terms: "The reader will see a double meaning. . . . . The reader won't understand." The clairvoyance of editors with respect to the thoughts and reactions of this lone reader is nothing less than preternatural. Embarrassingly, however, their psychic or telepathic finds are occasionally reversed by the higher editorial echelon, which not infrequently restores the analyst's original phrasing or something like it.*

- Kent: *Any reputable and studious man knows the good and evil of the ways of thought. No worthy soul consciously nourishes a prejudice or willfully flashes a cliché; everyone knows the virtues of open-mindedness; no one boasts imperviousness to a new thought. And yet even in the best minds curious derelictions occur.* (Kent was intimately familiar with "best minds" and "curious derelictions.")

The two characteristics of the journal that Sherman Kent par-

ticularly nurtured while he was at the helm were its comprehensiveness and its eclecticism. All aspects of collection were covered, from the clandestine acquisition of documents to technical collection and mining open sources. The challenges of analysis, including treatment of successes and failures, were highlighted. Covert and clandestine operations received a surprising amount of attention—of particular note were the articles by experienced officers on how to recruit, handle, and work with individuals from diverse cultures. *Studies'* readers were treated to articles on training, intelligence organization, management, even public relations. The journal looked at the handling of increasing amounts of information using new processes, including computers.[9] Reflecting newly uncovered information on historical intelligence operations, especially from World War II, there was a plethora (some might say an overabundance) of historical articles in *Studies*. So many valuable arti-

---

[9] At a time when a single computer could fill a room, an astonishingly prescient piece in 1960 predicted the day when "computers the size of a portable TV set will operate on wall socket power." Joseph Becker, "The Computer—Capabilities, Prospects, and Implications," *Studies* 4, no. 4 (Fall 1960).

cles on counterintelligence (CI) were published—significant, considering this also was the era of legendary CI chief James Angleton—that the CI staff reissued the collection separately as "Readings in Counterintelligence," in two volumes: 1957–64 and 1964–74.

If *Studies* had one failing during the Kent era, it was that the journal was less than successful at encouraging contributions from outside the CIA, even though it explicitly sought "the advice and participation of every member of the intelligence profession to do the job well."[10] Despite an abundance of articles on assessing foreign militaries, for example, few contributions came from the US military. *Studies* did run several articles by air force officers on the role of intelligence in air operations—but similar treatments by navy or army officers are absent.

In 1968, to honor Kent as he retired, the annual *Studies in Intelligence* award (given since 1960) was renamed. Today, the Sherman Kent Award, presented for "the most significant contribution to the literature of intelligence submitted to *Studies*," remains the Oscar of intelligence literature. Unlike the Oscars, however, it is not necessarily awarded every year, only when an article is deemed "sufficiently outstanding." In 16 years out of 45, no Kent Award has been given, a

---

[10] Editor's Introduction [prepared by Charles Lichenstein], *Studies*, January 1956.

record that underscores the high standards the journal's editor and editorial board have maintained.[11]

Life after Kent

Studies in Intelligence made few changes when Kent retired. The editorial board maintained a great deal of continuity well into the 1970s, first under Abbot Smith and then under Hugh Cunningham. And when Philip Edwards retired as editor, shortly after Kent left, that position likewise saw little change for almost a decade, first under Joseph Mathews and then Clinton Conger.

In general, the contents of the journal followed the same eclectic and comprehensive path set down by Kent.[12] There were still many contributions to the history of intelligence, but the plethora of articles on World War II matters dropped off somewhat. Thanks to a series of articles, many of them award-winning, by legendary imagery analyst Dino Brugioni, readers were treated to an informal course in making sense of overhead photography. Consistent with current events and readers' interests, there were

---

[11] In addition to the Kent prize, the editorial board presents some half dozen other awards for distinguished articles and book reviews each year, including one named after Walter Pforzheimer, for the best student submission.

[12] Kent's shadow continued to loom over *Studies*. In the 25th anniversary issue, for example, the retrospective written by Hal Ford was not on the journal so much as on its founder. Harold Ford, "A Tribute to Sherman Kent," *Studies* 24, no. 3 (Fall 1980).

increasing number of articles on Southeast Asia, in addition to the continuing treatment of matters Soviet and Chinese.

The change to an 8½-by-11–inch format in 1972 allowed greater flexibility for graphics. The first graphic representation in the journal had been a simple flowchart of analysis on the Soviet economy that appeared in the third issue (May 1956). Interestingly, the first maps had nothing to do with contemporary intelligence matters: The Winter 1958 issue ran high-quality, color representations of Robert E. Lee's invasion of Maryland in September 1862. *Studies* debuted the fold-out in an article on management of data for air targeting (Spring 1959): a targeting form used by Air Force analysts (and helpfully marked "Note: Target is Fictitious"). The next innovation, black and white photography, appeared in the following issue: a portrait of William Donovan, accompanying Allen Dulles's tribute to the recently deceased OSS director, along with photographic reproductions of letters between Donovan and President Franklin Roosevelt on the issue of centralized intelligence. Color reproductions of forged postal stamps brightened the Summer 1960 issue, and probably more than one reader took up a penknife in the spring of 1963 to remove the detailed, color, fold-out map of the China-India border region. By the mid-1960s, graphs, charts, diagrams, and photographs were standard fare, particularly for the more technical articles. Full color photography, however, had to wait until the Spring 1980 issue (this was not *LOOK* magazine, after all), with stunning photos of the engineering of the Glomar Explorer.[13]

In keeping with the intent of the journal to provide readers with the "best thinking" on diverse intelligence topics, *Studies* in the mid-1970s began to issue specially classified supplements to the regular issues, dealing with matters at the Top Secret Codeword level. These usually had to do with SIGINT or space imagery, although the supplement for the Summer 1973 issue comprised three articles, classified Secret, on early CIA history regarding the clandestine services. Some later *Studies* supplements published special studies commissioned by the Center for the Study of Intelligence, such as on US intelligence and Vietnam (1984).

---

[13] A ship outfitted to retrieve a sunken Soviet submarine.

> ❝
>
> **In the 1980s, *Studies* paid more attention to the subject of making analysis relevant for policymakers.**
>
> ❞

Content patterns relevant to various time periods can be detected. For example, despite the attempts to reach readers by publishing special supplements, the number of articles dropped off in the 1970s coincident with the Agency's "Time of Troubles" over public revelations and congressional inquiries into past CIA activities. Occasionally, an issue of the journal was even cancelled due to a dearth of quality submissions. Some issues had only three articles. Not surprisingly, counterintelligence pieces seem completely absent from this period. Also not surprisingly, beginning in the 1970s there was an increase in the number of articles dealing with such topics as legislative oversight, the CIA and the law, secrecy in a democracy, declassification, executive privilege, and the CIA's power of pre-publication review.

Into the 1980s

Studies articles in the 1980s paid more attention to the subject of making analysis—particularly political analysis—relevant for policymakers through improving the current intelligence and estimative processes as well as analytic tradecraft. In developing a literature on dealing with terrorism, the journal once more was helping prepare its readers for the future: Lance

Haus's treatment of the challenges of analyzing terrorism, particularly his warning not to confuse activity with productivity, seems prescient.[14] Similarly, Bruce Reidel's description of the institutional devil's advocate used by the Israeli military presaged wider discussion of the concept years later, especially in the wake of the 2001 terrorist attacks in New York and Washington.[15] Writers for *Studies* in the 1980s also focused on the phenomenon of burgeoning broadcast media—witness the several articles on the value of collecting open source material through television.

Another trend during the decade was the growth in the number of humorous pieces—tongue-in-cheek articles, funny vignettes,

---

[14] Lance Haus, "The Predicament of the Terrorism Analyst," *Studies* 29, no. 4 (Winter 1985).
[15] Bruce Reidel, "Communication to the Editor," *Studies* 30, no. 4 (Winter 1986).

amusing imagery, even some doggerel. One speculates that, after the travails of the 1970s, *Studies* served as a therapeutic outlet by becoming a vehicle for those who sought refuge in humor. The foundation for such pieces had been laid in the 1950s, beginning with an essay on the English language as a barrier to communication and a lead article on working with officials of another country that interspersed solid observations about the process with cross-cultural comments worthy of present-day humorist Bill Bryson.[16] Most of the light-hearted writing in *Studies*, however, appears in the post-Kent period. Of special note is the only article to have been reprinted twice after its initial publication: "Elegant Writing in the Clandestine Services," by "Richard Puderbaugh," who had good reason to stay anonymous.[17]

Humor, admittedly, is quite subjective, so one's favorites might not be another's. Nonetheless, hard-working readers who are world-weary and need some laughter are encouraged to seek refreshment in these refuges:

• Russ Bowen, "An Engineering Approach to Literature Appreciation" (Spring 1980): *By plotting the frequency distribution of the nominal or "best" ratings of the nearly 700 authors to whom the*

---

[16] Burney Bennett, "The Greater Barrier," *Studies* 2, no. 4 (Fall 1958).

[17] This article originally appeared in vol. 16, no. 1 (1972 Special Edition), was reprinted in the Fall 1980 issue, and appeared again in the spring of 1990. *Studies* is overdue to run it again.

> ❝
> **The 1980s also saw growth in the number of humorous pieces.**
> ❞

system has been applied, a bell-shaped curve results . . . . To an engineer this is suggestive of some kind of consistent mechanism at work. On the other hand, some may view this result as simply evidence of a degree of intolerance or snobbishness on my part.

• Robert Sinclair, "The CIA Canoe Pool" (Spring 1984): *A clothes brush at the office helps, but there are still days when I must try to maintain my dignity with patches of dried mud on the lower third of my trousers. Or spider webs.*

• Linda Lovett, "POEEDGR" (Winter 1986):
Once upon my desk computer, as I read my "VM Tutor,"

Studies' first wholly unclassified issue (1992).

Came a message from a userID I'd not seen before— While I nodded, nearly napping, this odd message came up, zapping All the input I'd been tapping, tapping in for hours before. . . .

• Roger Girdwood, "Burn Bags" (Summer 1989): *Some people never go to the burn bag chute. But they never have a full burn bag in their workplace, either . . . . When you arrive at work one morning, you discover a trove of 25 burn bags in the place where you thought you had a popcorn popper. Fortunately, you can usually identify this culprit by making a careful analysis of his or her bag-stapling technique. Like fingerprints and snowflakes, no two staple jobs are alike.*

• [And my personal favorite,] David Fichtner, "Taking Arms against a Sea of Enemies" (Summer 1992): *Hamlet has made no public protest over his uncle's succession . . . . Embassy reporting, however, states that there is a subversive campaign underway attacking the fundamental legitimacy of the current [Danish] government.*

Toward a New Century

Consistent with the journal's success in previous decades, *Studies* articles in recent years have reflected the times and helped prepare readers for changes ahead by challenging them to think in new ways. One prescient article in 1990 antici-

> ❝
> **In recent years,
> articles
> have challenged
> readers to think in new
> ways.**
> ❞

pated the effects the information revolution would have on intelligence analysis: "The future is now . . . . The DI will have to deal with three major challenges: the information age, the devaluation of intelligence, and a crisis of self-doubt"—a neat summation of the problems that the DI has faced over the past decade. Another fact of life in the Internet age was foreshadowed in Joseph Seanor's ground breaking article in 1992 on computer hacking.[18]

Among the typically cogent, thoughtful pieces covering a wide array of intelligence topics, some stand out and, in fact, make for chilling reading years later. Consider the opening line of Kevin Stroh's behind-the-scenes account of analysis on

Iraq's nuclear weapons: "CIA's assessment of Iraq's prewar nuclear weapons program was an intelligence failure." Remember, this was written *in 1995*. Stroh's article is key to understanding how intelligence on the same subject went wrong more recently, for in 1991 the CIA's failure was its assessment that Baghdad had *not* gone as far as it really had.[19]

Even more sobering is "The Coming Intelligence Failure," offered by Russ Travers of DIA in 1996:

> *The year is 2001 . . . . As had been true of virtually all previous intelligence failures, collection was not the issue. The data were there, but we had failed to recognize correctly [their] significance and put [them] in context . . . . From the vantage point of 2001, intelligence failure is inevitable. Despite our best intentions, the system is sufficiently dysfunctional that intelligence failure is guaranteed.[20]*

Prescience is rare, of course, and is seen exclusively in hindsight. For every good prediction in back issues that gives a shudder

today upon rereading, there probably was at least one wrong (but one hopes well-meaning and well-reasoned) assessment, such as the bold prediction in 1985, just as Gorbachev was coming to power in the USSR, that the passing of the old Soviet leadership "will not herald an era of major reforms . . . . The USSR will not experience anything approaching a genuine systemic crisis before the year 2000." Ah, well, it happens to everyone. But it is also certain that Sherman Kent would point out that displaying prescience is not the point. The value of *Studies in Intelligence* is in its presentation of principles of the trade—things that worked and did not—and its postulation of what might reasonably be. To the degree that readers of *Studies* have their imaginations engaged and stimulated with speculative pieces, the journal has done its job.

---

[18] Carmen Medina, "The DI Mission in the 21st Century," *Studies* 34, no. 4 (Winter 1990). Joseph Seanor, "The Hannover Hackers," *Studies* 36, no. 1 (Spring 1992).

[19] Kevin Stroh, "Iraq's Nuclear Weapons Program," *Studies* 39, no. 4 (Winter 1995).
[20] Russ Travers, "The Coming Intelligence Failure," *Studies* 40, no. 2 (1996).

> ## "
> ## More than 1,000 individuals have contributed articles to *Studies.*
> ## "

The Way Ahead

More than 1,000 individuals, from junior officers to Directors of Central Intelligence, and even an unwitting Soviet intelligence officer or two, have contributed articles to *Studies* over the years. A review reveals that, while the journal has many beloved writers of multiple articles, most contributors had just one excellent article in them—indeed, most of the memorable articles, I venture to generalize, were the single offering of one person who never wrote for *Studies* again (one hopes it was not because of the editing process). These included deputy directors of intelligence (Robert Amory, Ray Cline, Doug MacEachin), a future presidential adviser (William Bundy), a CIA inspector general (Fred Hitz), and a future Marine Corps commandant (P. X. Kelley). At the same time, *Stud-*

Studies and the Internet

With the advent of the Worldwide Web, CIA and *Studies* went public on a global scale. Introduced to cia.gov in 1995, unclassified issues of *Studies* and the unclassified articles extracted from classified issues are placed on the CIA Web site (under Center for the Study of Intelligence) not long after the journal is published in paper. Available on-line are issues back to 1992.

The site also includes an index of declassified articles available at the National Archives and Records Administration and a digital archive and index of about 600 other unclassified articles about the business of intelligence.

---

ies could not do without its serial contributors. The ten most prolific authors—Dino Brugioni, Jack Davis, Philip Edwards, Benjamin Fischer, Sherman Kent, Andrew Kobal, Henry Lowenhaupt, Donovan Pratt, Kevin Ruffner, Michael Warner—each wrote at least eight articles, and this listing does not include book reviews.

For the past 10 years or so—since about the time the *Studies* editorial board was opened to officers from the Intelligence Community at large—there has been an encouraging trend toward more submissions from outside the CIA, fully in keeping with the intent of Sherman Kent and the other founders of the journal. Much of this trend reflects the shift in civilian analytic and operational resources toward support of the military. Other developments will reinforce this tendency: the creation of the Director of National Intelligence and the demise of the DCI position; the widening of authorship of the *President's Daily Brief*; and the creation of national centers for counterterrorism, counterintelligence, and counterproliferation. Through interactions with CIA colleagues, more intelligence professionals are likely to become acquainted with *Studies in Intel-*

ligence, come to appreciate what it offers, and wish to contribute their perspectives to it. The current interagency editorial board encourages all intelligence officers to participate in that valuable accumulation of professional knowledge that is the main mission of *Studies*.

Another development faced by *Studies in Intelligence*—and, frankly, one with which the journal is still coming to grips—is the expansion of its readership beyond the province of the intelligence professional. For most of its history, *Studies* has published for the knowledgeable intelligence practitioner. With every other issue now unclassified and posted on the CIA Web site, and with many of its previously classified articles now declassified, *Studies* must consider its public, uncleared readers.[21] Should the journal devote special attention to this new audience? How can it best serve this new readership—Should it publish more basic, "primer" pieces? Should it produce a glossary for readers who are not intelligence professionals? Just how much background knowledge is it safe to assume? Is there a danger that *Studies* might counterproductively be suspected of acting as a public advocate for the intelligence profession, for a particular intelligence policy, or for any of the

---

[21] An accessible collection is Brad Westerfield, ed., *Inside CIA's Private World: Declassified Articles from the Agency's Internal Journal, 1955–1992* (New Haven, CT: Yale University Press, 1995).

agencies that compose the Intelligence Community? What other effects—positive and negative—might come from providing a subcorpus of intelligence literature to the general public? Will the journal be able to withstand potential pressures for self-censorship during this time of almost universal criticism of the performance of the Intelligence Community? Or is it more important than ever to provide a forum for scholarly debate about the intelligence profession?

Finally, the future of *Studies in Intelligence* is not isolated from that of the changing face of the Intelligence Community. The journal must reckon with its standing with the Director of National Intelligence, for example, especially as it continues to

> " The journal is still coming to grips with the expansion of its readership beyond intelligence professionals. "

embrace a less CIA-centric approach in favor of one more community-oriented. There can be no doubt that *Studies* will change as a result of the issues it faces today; it is equally certain that it will continue to serve, for it has become indispensable. Intelligence historians resident in the Center for the Study of Intelligence frequently respond to questions—often from very high levels—regarding whether an activity

has been tried before or a line of thinking raised before. One of the first sources they turn to is *Studies in Intelligence* and, as often as not, the answer lies in one of its 50 volumes—proof positive that Sherman Kent's dream of creating an intelligence literature has been achieved.

After 50 years, *Studies* is still accomplishing its mission of accumulating the "best thinking" of intelligence thinkers and practitioners. That mission has remained unchanged. As Sherman Kent remarked during *Studies'* 25th anniversary year: "The game still swings on the educated and thoughtful" intelligence officer.

The "Photo Gap" that Delayed Discovery of Missiles in Cuba

Max Holland

> " The Kennedy administration harbored three great secrets in connection with the Cuban missile crisis. "

Max Holland is the author of *The Kennedy Assassination Tapes* (New York: A. Knopf, 2004). He dedicates this article to the late Sam Halpern, a longtime CIA officer whom he interviewed for this study.

The Kennedy administration harbored three great secrets in connection with the October 1962 Cuban missile crisis, not just two, as widely understood.

The most sensitive, of course, was the *quid pro quo* that ended the acute phase of the crisis. In exchange for the prompt, very public, and verified withdrawal of Soviet missiles, President Kennedy publicly pledged not to invade Cuba and secretly committed to quietly dismantling Jupiter missile sites in Turkey in 1963. Management of this first secret was so masterful—involving public dissembling, private disinformation, and a plain lack of information—that the *quid pro quo* remained a lively, but unconfirmed, rumor for nearly three decades.

The second secret involved keeping a lid on Washington's ongoing effort to subvert Fidel Castro's regime. Operation MONGOOSE, which was overseen by Attorney General Robert Kennedy, played a significant role in fomenting the missile crisis. Yet that covert effort was not part of the public discourse in 1962 and remained a secret in this country until the mid-1970s. Only after an unprecedented Senate probe into intelligence activities did enough information seep out to reveal that Castro's fears of US military intervention (and Soviet claims to that effect) were not wholly unfounded, however mistaken.

It was the administration's third secret, however, that has proven the hardest to unpack. The Kennedy administration "shot itself in the foot" when it limited U-2 surveillance for five crucial weeks in 1962, which is why it took the government a full month to spot offensive missiles in Cuba.[1] If proven, this "photo gap," as it was dubbed by Republican critics, threatened to tarnish the image of "wonderfully coordinated and error-free 'crisis management'" that the White House sought to project before and after October 1962.[2] The administration's anxiety over whether cover stories about the gap might unravel even trumped, for a time, its concern over keeping secret the *quid pro quo*. After all, an oral assurance with the Soviets concerning the Jupiters could always be denied, while proof of the photo gap existed in

---

[1] Author's interview with Richard Lehman, 3 June 2003.

[2] McGeorge Bundy, *Danger and Survival* (New York: Random House, 1988), 459. Republicans coined the term "photo gap" after the infamous (and non-existent) "missile gap," which Democrats had exploited to good effect in 1960.

All statements of fact, opinion, or analysis expressed in this article are those of the author. Nothing in the article should be construed as asserting or implying US government endorsement of an article's factual statements and interpretations.

> ## " Liberals had been appalled by John McCone's appointment as DCI. "

the government's own files. Largely because the administration labored mightily to obfuscate the issue, the photo gap remains under-appreciated to this day, notwithstanding the vast literature on the missile crisis.[3]

Recently declassified documents finally permit history to be filled in 43 years after the crisis, and these same records alter the conventional story in at least one important respect. John McCone, the director of central intelligence (DCI), and the CIA as a whole were deeply distrusted by key administration officials in the weeks leading up to discovery of the missiles. Moreover, the rampant uncertainty that prevailed within the Agency, itself, has been downplayed, if not forgotten, to the detriment of depicting the complexity of what actually occurred. The literature on the crisis has painted a rosier-than-warranted picture of how human intelligence, assiduously collected in September, finally overcame self-imposed restrictions on U-2 overflights. What actually happened was not a textbook case of how the system should work. And although tension between the CIA and the administration abated after the crisis, it was not by very much. Lingering sensitivity over the photo gap left a chill in the relationship between the DCI and the Kennedy brothers, a result that can only be labeled ironic, given McCone's role in securing the critical photo coverage.

A New Leader at Langley

Little more than a year after the Bay of Pigs fiasco, and for the first time in its short history, the CIA was being led by a man who was widely viewed as being at direct odds with the administration he served—that is, if political affiliation or ideology counted for anything.

Liberals within the administration had been appalled by John McCone's appointment in September 1961, and not only because he was the stereotype of the wealthy, conservative Republican businessmen who had overwhelmingly populated the Eisenhower administration.[4] As chairman of the Atomic Energy Commission, McCone had acquired a reputation as a "militant" anti-communist and "real [bureaucratic] alley fighter," and he promised to be diametrically opposed to the dominant ethos of the Kennedy administration.[5] Indeed, here was a California engineer-turned-tycoon who would likely have been a strong candidate for secretary of defense had Richard Nixon won the 1960 election.[6]

Apart from being regarded with deep suspicion by Democrats because of his Republican ties, there was also the more specific concern that McCone's stiff-necked anti-communism might distort the intelligence produced by a demoralized CIA, still reeling from the failed invasion of Cuba.[7] Opponents of McCone's appointment had argued that he

---

[3] Explanations for and/or dismissals of the photo gap are as varied and voluminous as the literature on the missile crisis itself. A thorough historiography would be instructive, but is beyond the scope of this article. While short on details, the first account to grasp the gist and significance of the photo gap was Alexander George, *Deterrence in American Foreign Policy* (New York: Columbia University Press, 1974), 473–77. Peter Usowski provided an insightful account of McCone's role in "John McCone and the Cuban Missile Crisis," *International Journal of Intelligence and Counterintelligence* 2, no. 4 (Winter 1988). Important details later emerged in a history/memoir by CIA imagery analyst Dino Brugioni, *Eyeball to Eyeball* (New York: Random House, 1990). Official document compilations and a history separately released by the CIA began to build an authoritative record in the 1990s. See Mary McAuliffe, ed., *CIA Documents on the Cuban Missile Crisis* (Washington: Central Intelligence Agency, 1992); US Department of State, *Foreign Relations of the United States, 1961–1963, Vol. XI, Cuban Missile Crisis and Aftermath* (Washington: Government Printing Office, 1996), and *Foreign Relations of the United States, 1961–1963, Vol. X, Cuba 1961–1962* (Washington: Government Printing Office, 1997), hereafter *FRUSvX* and *FRUSvXI;* and Gregory Pedlow and Donald Welzenbach, *The CIA and the U-2 Program, 1954–1974* (Washington: Central Intelligence Agency, 1998). Still, several key documents have only been released over the past two years via the CIA Records Electronic Search Tool (CREST) at the National Archives-College Park (NARA).

[4] McCone had also served as Truman's under secretary of the Air Force during 1950–51.
[5] Roger Hilsman Oral History, 14 August 1970, John F. Kennedy Library (JFKL), 15.
[6] George Kistiakowsky, *A Scientist at the White House* (Cambridge, MA: Harvard University Press, 1976), 257.
[7] John McCone Oral History, 19 August 1970, Lyndon B. Johnson Library (LBJL), 7.

> ❝
> **McCone raised the specter of offensive missiles being emplaced.**
> ❞

would be in a position to dominate intelligence in a city where information is often power. Apprehension inside the CIA over the appointment matched the trepidation outside. McCone was virtually a novice with regard to the craft of intelligence, and inflicting an outsider on the CIA was considered an even graver punishment than saddling it with a dogmatic man known for his molten temper and "slide-rule mind."[8]

It was against this backdrop of doubt and distrust that an untested DCI faced his first real crisis late in the summer of 1962.

Cuba Heats Up

The first of two U-2 overflights of Cuba scheduled for August occurred on the fifth—too early, by a matter of days, to capture any telling evidence about what would soon be an unprecedented

Soviet military buildup on the island.[9] Reports from other sources, nonetheless, prompted McCone to raise the specter of offensive missiles being emplaced, during a Special Group Augmented (SGA) meeting on 10 August.[10]

McCone sounded the alarm again in Secretary of State Dean Rusk's office on 21 August, and while meeting with President Kennedy on 22 and 23 August. The Soviet Union was "in the red [behind in terms of nuclear missiles] and knew it," McCone reportedly averred, and thus Nikita Khrush-

chev was likely to try to redress that imbalance.[11] But the DCI did little to improve his persuasiveness, and much to enhance his Manichean reputation, when he promptly suggested staging a phony provocation against the US base at Guantánamo so that Washington would have a pretext for overthrowing Castro.[12] McCone was thought to be "too hard-line and suspicious," as Under Secretary of State George Ball later put it, besides being too cavalier about the relationship between Cuba and the East-West faceoff in Berlin.[13]

Following the 23 August meeting at the White House, McCone left for the West Coast, where the 60-year-old widower was to be married for the second time, before traveling to the French Riviera for his honeymoon. Altogether, the DCI planned to be away until late September. President Kennedy's advisers would later scorn the DCI for supposedly not warning the president before leaving, and/or for being absent during a critical period.[14] The first claim was demonstra-

---

[8] *Current Biography,* 1959, 274.

[9] Two overflights of Cuba per month—each of which traversed the island from west to east and back—had become the norm in the spring of 1962.

[10] The Special Group was a National Security Council subcommittee that oversaw all covert actions; the SGA dealt solely with Cuba.

---

[11] Brugioni, *Eyeball,* 96.

[12] Walter Elder, "John A. McCone: The Sixth Director of Central Intelligence," 1987, Box 1, CIA Miscellaneous Files, John F. Kennedy Assassination Records Collection, NARA, 45.

[13] George Ball, *The Past Has Another Pattern* (New York: Norton, 1982), 288.

[14] During a February 1965 interview with Robert Kennedy, Arthur Schlesinger, Jr., asked, "How much validity is there to [McCone's] feeling that he forecast the possibility of missiles in Cuba?" "None," answered the former attorney general. Edwin Guthman and Jeffrey Shulman, eds., *Robert Kennedy In His Own Words* (New York: Bantam Press, 1988), 15.

A U-2 on an operational mission.

> ## 66
> ## The president wanted the SA-2 information 'nailed right back into the box.'
> ## 99

bly false, but there probably was a marked difference between McCone's dispatch of the so-called "honeymoon cables" in September and actually having him in town, doggedly pressing his views. Still, as Sherman Kent, chairman of the CIA's Board of National Estimates, later observed, even if the DCI "had been in Washington and made a federal case of his intuitive guess . . . McCone would have had opposing him (1) the members of [the] US Intelligence Board [i.e., the Intelligence Community]; and (2) most presidential advisers including the four most important ones [who were experts on the Soviet Union]—[former ambassadors Charles] Bohlen, [Llewelyn] Thompson, [George] Kennan, and [serving

ambassador] Foy [Kohler]."[15] The president would have been far more likely to trust these four esteemed Kremlinologists, than to embrace the dissenting view of a "robber-baron Republican."[16]

On 29 August, the second scheduled overflight of the month finally occurred, after several

---

[15] Jack Davis, "Sherman Kent's Final Thoughts on Analyst-Policymaker Relations," *Sherman Kent Center for Intelligence Analysis: Occasional Papers* 2, no. 3 (June 2003): 9.

[16] Author's interview with Thomas Hughes, 2 July 2005.

delays due to bad weather. "I've got a SAM [surface-to-air missile] site," a photo interpreter reportedly shouted, minutes after the film was placed on a light table at the National Photographic Interpretation Center (NPIC), the specialized facility where U-2 film was taken for analysis.[17] The SAM proved to be an SA-2, the same missile that had caused Francis Gary Powers's U-2 to plummet to earth in the USSR in 1960. Soon, it appeared, the CIA would not be able to overfly Cuba with impunity. After being briefed, McCone reportedly observed, "They're not putting them in to protect the cane cutters. They're putting them in to blind our reconnaissance eye."[18] For virtually every other senior official and analyst, however, the deployment "came not as a shock, but as a problem to be dealt with deliberately."[19] The same missile had been sent previously to other Soviet client states in the Third World.

President Kennedy was inclined to believe the majority view: that the Soviet military aid was for

---

[17] Brugioni, *Eyeball*, 104.

[18] Ibid., 105. It has been said that McCone was "right but for the wrong reasons." The Soviet plan did call for the SA-2s to be ready before offensive missiles were operational, although for the sole purpose of defending them against an air attack. Khrushchev wrongly believed the missiles could be camouflaged. Anatoli Gribkov and William Smith, *Operation ANADYR* (Chicago, IL: Edition Q, 1994), 16, 28, 40, 51–52.

[19] Memorandum for DCI from Richard Lehman, "CIA Handling of the Soviet Build-up in Cuba, 1 July–16 October 1962" (hereafter Lehman Report), 14 November 1962, CREST, NARA, 12.

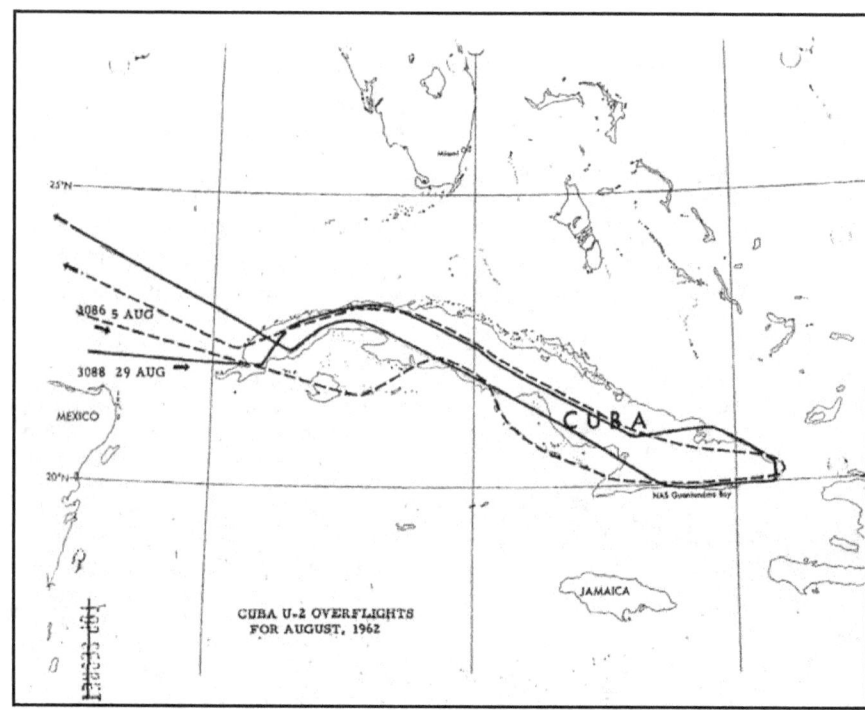

Figure 1: The flight paths of the two missions flown in August, both of which traversed the island.

the purpose of defending Cuba, while setting up the island as a model of socialist development and a bridgehead for subversive activities in the hemisphere.[20]

Consequently, the SA-2 deployment did not signal a foreign policy crisis in his eyes as much as it marked the onset of a domestic one. With a midterm election fast approaching, internal political pressure to "do something" about Cuba was bound to mount and had to be managed.[21] On 1 September, the president informed the acting DCI, Lt. Gen. Marshall "Pat" Carter, that he wanted the SA-2 information "nailed right back into the box" until such time as the White House decided to make it public.[22] Simultaneously, the president became greatly concerned about aerial reconnaissance of Cuba, and he was not satisfied until assured by the Joint Chiefs

---

> **"**
>
> ## The State Department looked askance at U-2 missions over sovereign airspace.
>
> **"**

that flights by the US military would not be conducted in a provocative manner.[23] These precautions left the vexing issue of intrusive U-2 surveillance twice a month unaddressed, though not for long.

Disagreement over the U-2

The next scheduled U-2 mission, on 5 September, detected additional SAM sites. Coincidentally, the "growing danger to the birds," as acting DCI Carter described it in a cable to McCone, was underscored by two distant events.[24] On 30 August, an air force U-2 had violated Soviet airspace for nine minutes during an air-sampling reconnaissance mission; then, on 9 September, a U-2 manned by a Taiwan-based pilot was lost over mainland China. These bookends to the first September overflight of Cuba provided new ammunition to critics of intrusive U-2 surveillance. One longstanding opponent was the State Department, which looked askance at U-2 missions over sovereign airspace. Now the department had a new ally: the White House.

On 10 September, the issue came to a head. At 10:00 a.m.,

McGeorge Bundy, the national security adviser, made an out-of-channel request to James Reber, chairman of the Committee on Overhead Reconnaissance (COMOR), the interagency committee charged with developing surveillance requirements for the U-2. Within 30 minutes, Bundy wanted answers to three questions:

- *How important is it to our intelligence objectives that we overfly Cuban soil?*

- *How much would our intelligence suffer if we limited our reconnaissance to peripheral activity utilizing oblique photography?*

- *Is there anyone in the planning of these missions who might want to provoke an incident?*[25]

COMOR members found the third question so provocative that they wondered if they were really expected to comment on it.[26] But it genuinely represented resentments festering within the administration after the Bay of Pigs. Reflecting the president's own jaundiced view, Bundy and Rusk believed that the CIA and the Pentagon had put Kennedy in an unforgivable bind before and during the agency-designed invasion of Cuba in April 1961. The two men, moreover, had been criticized severely for their own passivity at the time. Bundy

---

[20] *FRUSvX*, 942–43, 964, 969–70.

[21] Bundy, *Danger*, 393, 413.

[22] Telephone Conversation between Marshall Carter and Carl Kaysen, 1 September 1962, CREST, NARA. Inhibitions placed on the distribution of intelligence provide a telling measure of how the crisis was initially perceived. By late August, the CIA was not including raw intelligence about the Cuban buildup in community-wide publications unless it had been corroborated by NPIC. The president's 1 September injunction made this practice official, although Carter pretended that he, rather than "higher authority," had imposed the clampdown on this "forbidden subject." Distribution of raw intelligence was normal until 12 October, when it was restricted to US Intelligence Board members. Ibid., and Director of Central Intelligence, "Report to the President's Foreign Intelligence Advisory Board on Intelligence Community Activities Relating to the Cuban Arms Build-up: 14 April Through 14 October 1962" (hereafter PFIAB Report), 26 December 1963, CREST, NARA, 48–53.

[23] *FRUSvX*, 1023–24.

[24] McAuliffe, ed., *CIA Documents*, 47.

[25] Memorandum for the Record, "Telephone Conversation with Mr. Tom Parrott on 10 September Concerning IDEALIST Operations Over Cuba," 10 September 1962, CREST, NARA.

[26] Ibid.

> ## "
> ## When men of rank involve themselves in planning [U-2] tracks, good intelligence officers just listen.
> ## "

and Rusk were thus hyper-sensitive about protecting the president from anything that smacked of another trap, especially when high-ranking military and intelligence officials were scarcely concealing their determination to force the president "to atone for his restraint" during the 1961 operation.[27]

When Reber pleaded for more time to prepare his answers, a high-level meeting was scheduled for 5:45 p.m. in Bundy's White House office. In the meantime, shortly before 3:00 p.m., the national security adviser rescinded approval of the remaining September overflight, presumably to demonstrate that he was dead serious.[28]

Rusk tried to open the unusual meeting with a bit of levity. Nodding to Marshall Carter, whom he had known since World War II, Rusk said, "Pat, don't you ever let me up? How do you expect me to negotiate on Berlin with all these [U-2] incidents?" As was his habit whenever Rusk advocated a cautious course, Robert Kennedy immediately snapped, "What's the matter, Dean, no guts!"[29] The palpable tension between these two men almost overshadowed the substance of the meeting. "Let's sustain the overflights and the hell with the

international issues," Kennedy reportedly advocated.[30]

But the secretary of state worried that a U-2 incident would provoke two simultaneous uproars, one domestic and one foreign—the former arguing for an invasion and the latter condemning the United States worldwide. Soviet propaganda had successfully

managed "to turn U-2 into a kind of dirty word," as one columnist later put it.[31] International opinion regarded the overflights as "illegal and immoral," and even Washington's staunchest allies found them unpalatable.[32] Rusk shrewdly argued that losing a U-2 over Cuba would compromise Washington's unquestioned right to fly it in international waters along Cuba's periphery, and, given Cuba's narrowness, maybe offshore flights were sufficient anyway. COMOR experts said that that meant interior areas of Cuba were unlikely to be covered.

---

[27] McCone's August proposal about staging an incident at Guantánamo reflected the "invasion-minded mentalities" prevalent in intelligence and military circles. Hughes interview.

[28] DD/R Memo for the Record, "Cuban Overflights," 10 September 1962, CREST, NARA.

[29] *FRUSvX,* 1054–55.

[30] Brugioni, *Eyeball,* 137.

---

[31] C. L. Sulzberger, "The Villain Becomes a Hero," *New York Times,* 12 November 1962.

[32] Brugioni, *Eyeball,* 136; Hughes interview.

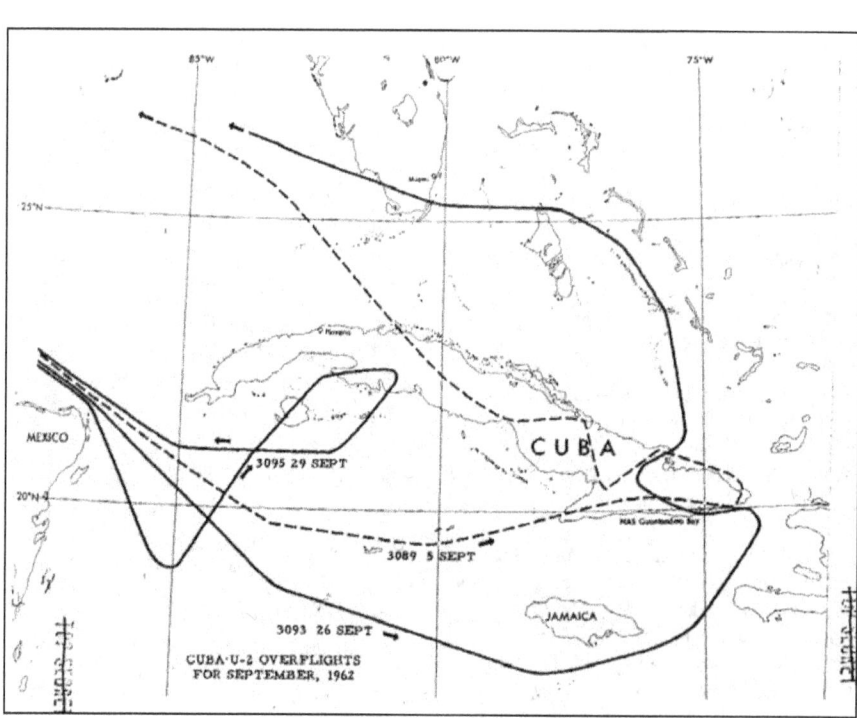

Figure 2: Only the 5 September mission, shown here, spent an extended amount of time in Cuban airspace. The paths of the following four flights (here and Figure 3) effectively precluded coverage of western Cuba and interior areas.

"Well, let's just give it a try," Rusk reportedly remarked."[33]

COMOR representatives were at a serious disadvantage. Not only were they in the uncomfortable position of dealing directly with officials who far outranked them, but, in place of McCone, the Agency was represented by Carter, who lacked the DCI's fearlessness and stature. Once administration officials began drawing up flight paths that avoided known SAM sites, the experts retreated. "When men of such rank involve themselves in planning mission tracks, good intelligence officers just listen," Reber later observed.[34] Finally,

> ## The result was a dysfunctional surveillance regime in a dynamic situation.

in light of Bundy's steadfast support of Rusk and Robert Kennedy's acquiescence, Carter agreed to a Rusk proposal to reinstate the canceled September overflight, but as four separate missions: two flights that would remain in international waters and two that would go "in-and-out" over small portions of central and eastern Cuba.[35]

The next morning, President Kennedy approved the schedule of what were called (technically, but misleadingly) "additional" flights.[36] The political decision to desist from intrusive or risky overflights and stretch out the missions would be doubly crippling because of an uncontrollable (yet foreseeable) factor, namely, the vagaries of Caribbean weather from September to November, when the region is beset by torrential rains and hurricanes. Because approvals for overflights were hard to come by, the CIA made a habit of husbanding U-2 missions. It was an operational practice to abort any mission if the weather was forecast to be more than 25 percent overcast.[37] Consequently, the 10 September decision not only limited the photographic "take" from every overflight, but had the unanticipated effect of drastically stretching out the mission schedule.[38] The result was a dysfunctional surveillance regime in a dynamic situation. Figures 1–3 depict the changes that flowed from the decision to degrade the primary tool used to verify Soviet capabilities in Cuba.[39]

It was during this very period, of course, that offensive missiles

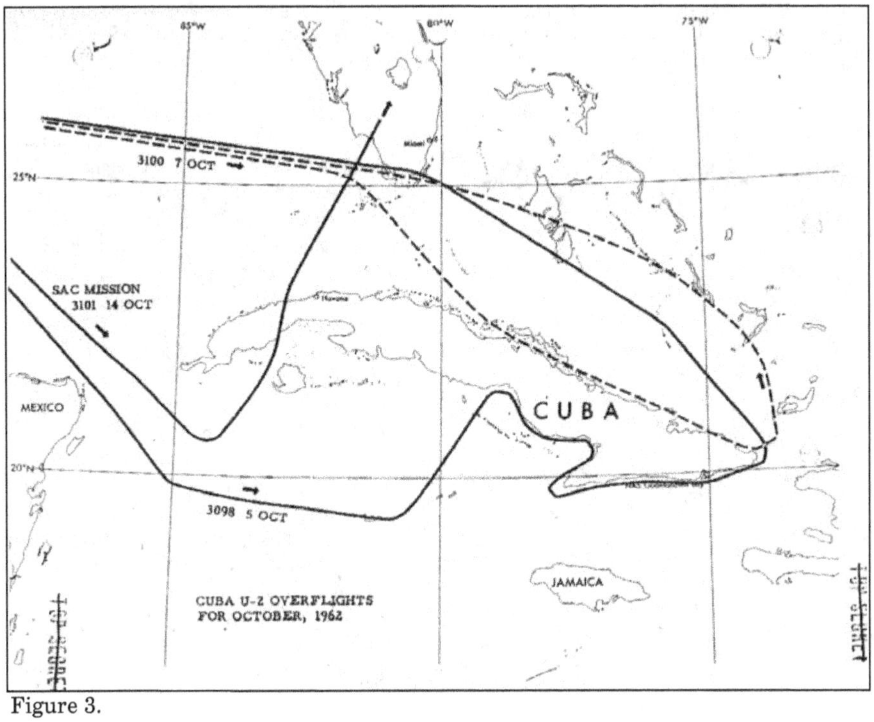

---

[33] Brugioni, *Eyeball*, 136. One expert remarked after the meeting, "After all this time and the many photographs that had been shown to Secretary Rusk, I was surprised to see how stupid he was on reconnaissance." Ibid.

[34] Ibid., 138.
[35] *FRUSvX*, 1054. Carter had gone into the meeting not only intent on reinstating the second September overflight, but also hoping to add a third extended mission before the end of the month. Ibid.

[36] Memorandum for DD/R, "Status of Cuban Mission Approvals," 11 September 1962, CREST, NARA.
[37] Pedlow and Welzenbach, *U-2 Program*, 205.
[38] President Kennedy always insisted that the CIA complete the schedule of approved missions before requesting new overflights. Richard Helms, with William Hood, *A Look Over My Shoulder* (New York: Random House, 2003), 212.
[39] George, *Deterrence*, 477.

Figure 3.

> ## "
> ## The DCI did not realize the degree to which overflights had been attenuated until 24 September.
> ## "

began to arrive.[40] Recognizable equipment reached the vicinity of San Cristóbal on 17–18 September, and that was subsequently fixed as the earliest date after which U-2 surveillance might have gathered evidence of surface-to-surface missiles (SSMs) in Cuba.[41] Yet Washington, by denying itself the "hard information that a constant aerial surveillance would have revealed," as McCone later put it, did not establish the missiles' presence near San Cristóbal until nearly a full month later—15 October.[42]

Langley's Unease

Acting DCI Carter remonstrated on at least one occasion about the attenuation of U-2 surveillance. "We cannot put a stop to collection," fumed Carter during a US Intelligence Board meeting on 19 September. "Otherwise, the president would never know when the point of decision was reached."[43] Yet Carter proved incapable of reversing the decision, especially after a 19 September Special National Intelligence Estimate (SNIE) reaffirmed the conventional wisdom.[44] The presumption was that even if the Soviets dared to introduce SSMs, against all estimates, that would only occur after the SA-2 defense system was complete, which still appeared some weeks away.[45] Later, an Agency officer reportedly observed, perhaps harshly, that the acting DCI was "standing in quicksand which was hardening into concrete," but did not even realize it.[46]

The moment when McCone learned about changes in the surveillance regime remains vague to this day. The pace of cable traffic between Langley, Virginia, and Cap Ferrat on the French Riviera was so torrential that a wit in the cable section reportedly observed, "I have some

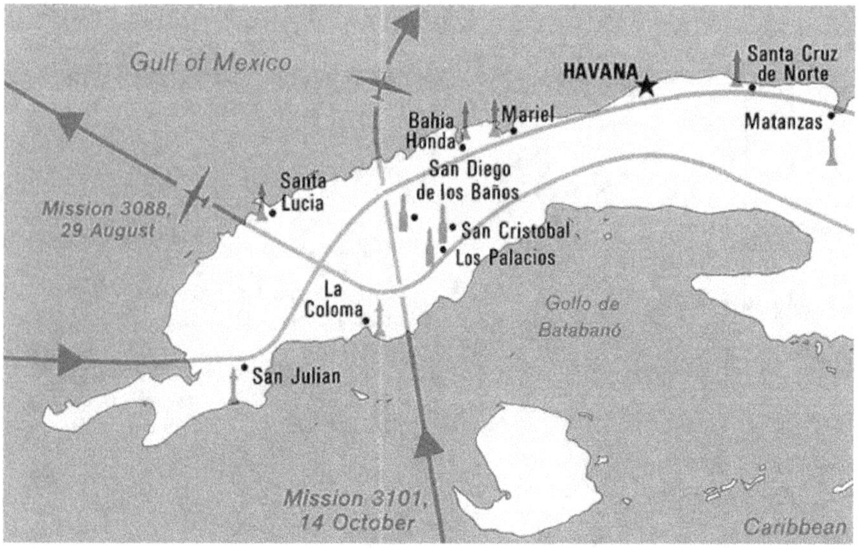

[40] CIA/Office of Research and Reports, "Cuba 1962: Khrushchev's Miscalculated Risk," 13 1964, National Security File, Country File: Cuba, Box 35, LBJL, 2–3.
[41] Lehman Report, 21.
[42] McCone Oral History, LBJL, 12.

[43] McAuliffe, ed., *CIA Documents,* 42. At this meeting, Maj. Gen. Robert Breitweiser, the Air Force's chief of intelligence, wondered if a pilotless "Firefly drone" might substitute for the U-2. Someone around the table immediately suggested that "Remember the Drone" would not be as gripping a battle cry as "Remember the Maine" had been in 1898. Hughes interview.

[44] On 20 September, Carter asked for a reconsideration of the 10 September decision, but Rusk easily deflected Carter's effort. "Thursday, 20 September [1962], Acting," CREST, NARA.
[45] Lehman Report, 17, 30. Measuring the electronic reaction to reconnaissance of Cuba was one of the National Security Agency's top priorities following the discovery of the SA-2s. On 15 September, NSA collected the first signals from a SPOON REST target acquisition radar, an advanced kind associated with the SA-2. "Handwritten draft of DIRNSA Note on Reporting Priorities," 10 October 1962, and "New Radar Deployment in Cuba," 19 September 1962, Cuban Missile Crisis Document Archive, NSA, http://www.nsa.gov/cuba/cuba00010.cfm. When not tied into an integrated command-and-control system, however, one SA-2 was practically incapable of shooting down a high-speed target acquired on its own radar. An integrated system was not turned on until late in October. According to Gen. Gribkov, Soviet commanders were not allowed to activate the system earlier because the SAMs had been emplaced to defend against an air attack against the missiles, not reconnaissance aircraft. Gribkov and Smith, *ANADYR,* 52.
[46] Unidentified officer, quoted in Brugioni, *Eyeball,* 139.

Figure 4: Soviet missile emplacements.

> ❝
> ## McCone was unable to reverse the administration's 'near-crippling caution.'
> ❞

doubts that the old man knows what to do on a honeymoon."[47] Yet the abrupt alteration in the U-2 regime went unmentioned in the cables, and McCone did not realize the degree to which overflights had been attenuated until he returned to Washington on 24 September.[48] Still, he was sufficiently concerned about the administration's lassitude to button-hole Bundy in late September while the national security adviser was in Europe for a NATO function. During a morning walk in Paris, the DCI zeroed in on what would turn out to be the Achilles' heel of the latest SNIE: the presumption that Moscow would not embrace such a risk in Cuba. Bundy was immovable, believing, as he did, that McCone was too fixated on a single element of the geo-political struggle, the thermonuclear balance.[49] The national security adviser remained determined not to allow McCone to entrap President Kennedy into sanctioning overflights with impunity. Any shootdown would become a *casus belli* for those who were itching to invade the island.

McCone met with President Kennedy and the attorney general privately on 26 September, shortly after returning to Wash-

ington but apparently was unable to reverse the administration's "near-crippling caution," as Richard Helms later termed it, until the approved overflight schedule had at least run its course.[50] Meanwhile, and to McCone's consternation, the photographic "take" from the attenuated U-2 missions was being cited to rebut the administration's increasingly vocal critics in Congress and the media.[51] Simultaneously, influential columnists like Walter Lippmann and James Reston, drawing from public testimony and/or private conversations with administration officials, were characterizing the surveillance of Cuba as "elaborate" or "total" in their columns.[52]

By early October, McCone was determined to remove the strictures on U-2 surveillance as a matter of principle, believing

that the CIA had already been "remiss" in settling for much less than complete coverage.[53] Coincidentally, NPIC chief Arthur Lundahl had asked his staff to develop a visual representation of photo surveillance of Cuba since early September. The map graphically depicted, at one glance, that large portions of Cuba had not been photographed since late August. The DCI "nearly came out of his chair when he saw the map," according to Lundahl.[54] "I'll take this," McCone reportedly said, apparently intending to make it exhibit number one at the SGA meeting to be chaired by Robert Kennedy on 4 October.[55]

Generally, the DCI and the attorney general were of like mind when it came to Cuba. But McCone's imputation of hesitancy on the administration's part echoed what several Republicans, especially Senator Kenneth Keating (R-New York), were asserting virtually every day in Congress, and the attorney general visibly bristled at the characterization.[56] When the subject turned specifically to the matter of the self-imposed reconnaissance blinders, McCone stressed

---

[47] Ibid., 97.

[48] As late as December 1962, the DCI remained perplexed about exactly what had happened during his absence. "I do not have an explanation of this and I'd like to know where this change in procedure came from, by whose order, and under what circumstances." McCone, "Notes for Mr. Earman," 17 December 1962, CREST, NARA.

[49] Bundy, *Danger*, 419–20.

[50] No minutes of the 26 September meeting are extant, but this may have been when McCone made a "strong representation to President Kennedy to remove some of the restraints on operations over Cuba," according to Richard Helms. *FRUSvX*, 1094–95, and Helms, *Shoulder*, 212. McCone also had an unrecorded conversation with the president on 8 October, and may have pressed his case then. James Giglio, "Kennedy on Tape," *Diplomatic History* 27, no. 5 (November 2003): 749.

[51] The Cuban buildup "is a configuration of defensive capability," Rusk confidently said during a rare, nationally televised interview on 29 September. David Larson, ed., *The "Cuban Crisis" of 1962* (Boston, MA: Houghton Mifflin, 1963), 28.

[52] Walter Lippmann, "On War Over Cuba," the *Washington Post*, 9 October 1962; and James Reston, "On Cuba and Pearl Harbor—the American Nightmare," *New York Times*, 12 October 1962. Rusk intensely disliked both columnists, so their private source was almost certainly Bundy, acting on President Kennedy's instructions. Hughes interview.

[53] McCone, "Notes for Mr. Earman," 17 December 1962, CREST, NARA.

[54] Brugioni, *Eyeball*, 159.

[55] Ibid.

[56] *FRUSvXI*, 12.

> ## "
> ## No one was keen to take responsibility for the gaping hole in coverage.
> ## "

that they were ill-advised, particularly since the SAMs were "almost certainly not operational."[57] McCone, presumably after pointing to Lundahl's map,

noted to the Special Group that there had been no coverage of the center of Cuba and more particularly, the entire western end of the Island for over a month, and all flights since 5 September had been either peripheral or limited and therefore CIA did not know, nor could advise, whether an offensive capability was being created. DCI objected strenuously to the limitations which had been placed on overflights and there arose a considerable discussion (with some heat) as to whether limitations had or had not been placed on CIA by the Special Group.[58]

Now that the gaping hole in coverage was becoming obvious, no one was very keen to take responsibility for it. The SGA as a body, of course, had not issued an edict in writing against intrusive overflights. Rather, under duress from Rusk and Bundy—neither of whom was in attendance now—the CIA and COMOR had desisted from submitting such requests after being told, in effect, that such flight paths, if proposed, would not be approved.[59] Indeed, the president could technically claim (and, on his behalf, Bundy later would) that he had approved every over-

flight request received since the SA-2s were discovered in late August.[60]

Making Headway

The 4 October meeting began nudging the surveillance regime in the direction that McCone was determined to move it. "It was the consensus that we could not accept restrictions which would foreclose gaining all reasonable knowledge of military installations in Cuba," McCone recorded in his memo of the meeting.[61] But the State Department, for one, was not going to yield that easily. Rusk's alter ego, Deputy Under Secretary of State U. Alexis Johnson, still managed to win agreement for a National Reconnaissance Office (NRO) report on an overall surveillance program for Cuba, to be presented at the next SGA meeting on 9 October.[62] That meant sev-

eral more days lost while the NRO pondered whether there was a substitute for the U-2. Nor was it clear that the White House would ultimately agree to remove the strictures on U-2 overflights, as became obvious on the next day, when McCone met with Bundy privately to discuss Cuba. The White House still viewed the unprecedented buildup as a domestic, rather than foreign policy, crisis.[63]

Separately from McCone's effort to lift restrictions on principle, CIA officers at the operational level were correlating new human intelligence reports about alleged missiles in Cuba. One report dated 7 September, in particular, had grabbed the attention of Ted Shackley, chief of the CIA's station in Miami, and officers in Task Force W, the MONGOOSE component at CIA headquarters. The report was from a Cuban observer agent, the lowest rank in the intelligence pecking order, who had been recruited under MONGOOSE.[64] In secret writing, the agent had conveyed information about a mountainous area near San Cristóbal, approximately 60 miles west of Havana, where "very secret and important work," believed to involve mis-

---

[57] Pedlow and Welzenbach, *U-2 Program*, 206.

[58] McAuliffe, ed., *CIA Documents*, 16.

[59] Lehman Report, 13; McCone, "Notes for Mr. Earman," 17 December 1962, CREST, NARA.

[60] "With respect to overflight policy, we [Bundy, Rusk, McNamara, McCone] agreed that all flights requested of the President were authorized by him," Bundy wrote in a February 1963 "Eyes Only" memo for these four officials. This effort to put senior officials on the same page with respect to any congressional inquiries also observed that "delays in executing approved [U-2] reconnaissance missions were not reported upward, or monitored downward." *FRUSvXI*, 703–4.

[61] *FRUSvXI*, 13.

[62] U. Alexis Johnson, *The Right Hand of Power* (Englewood Cliffs, NJ: Prentice-Hall, 1984), 381; Pedlow and Welzenbach, *U-2 Program*, 206; McAuliffe, ed., *CIA Documents*, 136.

[63] This meeting was also tense. McCone said that restrictions on U-2 flights "had placed the United States intelligence community in a position where it could not report with assurance the development of offensive capabilities in Cuba." Bundy took refuge in expert opinion, stating that he "felt the Soviets would not go that far," and the national security adviser "seemed relaxed" over the lack of hard information (or so McCone thought). McAuliffe, ed., *CIA Documents*, 115.

> **[To work around the politics,] CIA let DIA take the lead during the debate over resuming overflights.**

siles, was in progress.[65] Besides providing coordinates for a specific area, what made this agent's report intriguing was that it coincided with two refugee reports that described large missiles last seen heading west from Havana.[66]

Under normal circumstances, Task Force W officers would have simply funneled the human intelligence up to COMOR, where a new requirement could be fashioned. But since 10 September, enormous uncertainty, and even a kind of defensiveness, had developed within the CIA over U-2 flights—so much so, that Sam Halpern, Task Force W's executive officer, believed it advisable to avoid having only the CIA's fingerprints on the intelligence. He worried about it being discounted as the product of a politicized, overly aggressive, or simply unreliable Agency.[67]

Consequently, in late September, Col. John Wright, head of the MONGOOSE component at

the Defense Intelligence Agency (DIA), was invited to a briefing in Task Force W's war room. Based on the coordinates provided by the MONGOOSE agent, CIA officers in Task Force W had marked off a trapezoid-shaped area on a map, and they asked Wright to push a request for U-2 surveillance up his chain of command. The maneuver "got us [CIA] out of the line of fire and let DIA take the lead" during "days of fighting" in early October about an overflight, recalled Halpern.[68] There was, however, a potential bureaucratic downside: If a U-2 overflight found anything, Col. Wright and the very junior DIA would forever be credited with having astutely assembled the crucial intelligence.[69]

On 9 October, the SGA met again to consider U-2 surveillance. By this time, the last two missions authorized on 11 September had flown—on 5 and 7 October—without finding any evidence of offensive missiles.[70] McCone came to the meeting armed with

a quick paper, prepared by the Office of National Estimates, on the consequences of a presidential declaration stating that the Soviet buildup necessitated invasive reconnaissance of Cuba.[71] The DCI had also taken the precaution of inviting along an air force colonel who could testify about the vulnerability of a U-2 during an intrusive sweep of Cuba. The SA-2 sites were fully equipped by now, but from the American perspective they were still not functioning as an integrated SAM system.[72] Col. Jack Ledford, head of the CIA's Office of Special Activities, "presented a vulnerability analysis that estimated the odds of losing a U-2 over Cuba at 1 in 6."[73]

During the SGA meeting, no one single-mindedly maintained that the 10 September restrictions had to be lifted to allow photo coverage of a suspected surface-to-surface missile site.[74] On the basis of DIA's urgent recommendation, the COMOR had simply put the San Cristóbal area at the top of its target list *if* overflights of western Cuba were approved.[75] Ultimately, the SGA's recommendation to the president (which he approved promptly) eased the restrictions on overflights but by

[64] The White House and State Department were critical of the CIA's apparent inability to collect high-value human intelligence on Cuba and its corresponding dependence on technical means such as the U-2. Hughes interview. Helms observed in 1997 that this single piece of human intelligence was the sole "positive and productive" aspect of MONGOOSE. Ted Shackley, with Richard Finney, *Spymaster* (Dulles, VA: Potomac Books, 2005), 63.
[65] McAuliffe, ed., *CIA Documents*, 103–4.
[66] Ibid., 107–9; "Chronology of Specific Events Relating to the Military Buildup in Cuba" (hereafter PFIAB Chronology), undated, compiled for the President's Foreign Intelligence Advisory Board, 38, http://www.gwu.edu/~nsarchiv/nsa/cuba_mis_cri/chron.htm.
[67] Author's interview with Sam Halpern, 3 May 2003.

[68] Ibid, and interview of Halpern in Ralph Weber, ed., *Spymasters* (Wilmington, DE: Scholarly Resources, 1999), 125. DIA's request informed memos submitted to the COMOR, USIB, and NRO in early October.
[69] John Hughes, with A. Denis Clift, "The San Cristóbal Trapezoid," *Studies in Intelligence* (Winter 1992): 44–45.

[70] The 7 October peripheral overflight skirted what would turn out to be the SSM complexes in central Cuba, but photo-interpreters were unable to detect any sites, presumably because of the oblique coverage.
[71] McAuliffe, ed., *CIA Documents*, 119–22.
[72] CIA/Office of Research and Reports, "Miscalculated Risk," 28.
[73] Pedlow and Welzenbach, *U-2 Program*, 207. The odds cited likely pertained to an extended overflight of Cuba.

> ## It was a 'moment of splendor' for the U-2, its camera, and the photo-interpreters.

the most incremental margin imaginable.[76] Only one "in-and-out" flight over western Cuba was sanctioned.[77] If this initial mission "did not provoke an SA-2 reaction," additional in-and-out flights over western Cuba would be proposed, until a full mosaic of that region was obtained.[78]

The track of the mission approved on 9 October was plotted to include coverage of the San Cristóbal trapezoid. The overflight did not actually occur until 14 October, owing to inclement weather forecasts and the time needed to train an air force pilot in the intricacies of the more powerful U-2s operated by the CIA.[79] But eventually, Maj. Richard Heyser piloted the U-2 that took 928 photographs in six minutes over an area of Cuba that had not been photographed for 45 days.[80] The film was rushed to Suitland, Maryland, for processing and arrived at NPIC on the morning of 15 October. Shortly before 4:00 p.m., the CIA photo-interpreter on a team of four analysts announced, "We've got MRBMs [medium range ballistic missiles] in Cuba."[81] It was a "moment of splendor" for the U-2, its cameras and film, and the photo-interpreters, as Sherman Kent later put it, if not the CIA's finest hour of the Cold War.[82] The president issued blanket authority for unrestricted U-2 overflights on 16 October, and the missile crisis commenced in earnest.

Success or Failure?

Ultimately, the performance of the Intelligence Community has to be judged a success, albeit by a narrow margin.[83] The fact that the SSMs were detected and

---

[74] "I feel it would be erroneous to give the impression this [14 October] flight went where it went because we suspected [SSMs] were there. This was simply not the case." McCone, "Notes for Mr. Earman," 17 December 1962, CREST, NARA. McCone was apparently loath to make missions or flight paths contingent on human intelligence reports, since he was dead-set on lifting restrictions on principle. The logic behind the SGA's recommendation may have been perceived differently by others. The newly minted chairman of the Joint Chiefs of Staff, Gen. Maxwell Taylor, was acutely aware of the San Cristóbal trapezoid. He had been briefed by Col. Wright by 1 October. *FRUSvXI*, 1, note.

[75] PFIAB Chronology, 39–41; Lehman Report, 30–31; PFIAB Report, 75–77. A COMOR memorandum prepared on 5 October stated that the military items "of most immediate concern are the missile installations springing up all over the island." These were identified, in order, as known and suspected SAM sites; coastal cruise missile installations; and, third, SSM sightings that required confirmation or denial. Memo for USIB, "Intelligence Justification for U-2 Overflight of Cuba," 5 October 1962, CREST, NARA.

[76] Pedlow and Welzenbach, *U-2 Program,* 207.

[77] PFIAB Report, 32, 75–77.

[78] Pedlow and Welzenbach, *U-2 Program,* 207.

INITIAL IDENTIFICATION OF MRBM MISSILES IN CUBA
MRBM LAUNCH SITE 1
SAN CRISTOBAL, CUBA
14 OCTOBER, 1962

MISSILES

Convoy

---

[79] Because the administration was anxious to preserve "plausible deniability" in case of an incident, responsibility for the U-2 mission was shifted from the CIA to the Strategic Air Command. A cover story involving a regular air force pilot was deemed marginally more credible and signified how dread of another U-2 incident was still greater than any concern about new reports of SSMs. Pedlow and Welzenbach, *U-2 Program,* 207–9.

[80] *FRUSvXI*, 29.

[81] Brugioni, *Eyeball,* 200.

[82] Sherman Kent, "A Crucial Estimate Relived," *Studies in Intelligence* (Spring 1964): 115.

" The photo gap was more significant than the consistently wrong estimates. "

reported before any of them were perceived as operational was vital to the resolution that followed. Washington had precious days to deliberate, and then orchestrate a reaction short of an instant military attack. That decision shifted the onus of using force onto the Soviets. And once having seized the initiative via a quarantine, the Kennedy administration never lost it. Khrushchev, meanwhile, was denied the *fait accompli* he had tried to achieve by deception and was forced to improvise in a situation for which he had not planned sufficiently, if at all.

It has been argued, therefore, that the system basically worked. "Fortunately, the decision to look harder was made in time, but it would have been made sooner if we had listened more attentively to McCone," was the formulation McGeorge Bundy presented in his 1988 history/memoir.[84] This "system worked" view has been endorsed by every participant in the crisis who has written a memoir, as well as by most scholars of the crisis.[85] And it may well be that, given the intangibles of human behavior, the most one can ever expect is a kind of dogged performance by an intelligence service that somehow man-

ages, in the end, to prevent a strategic surprise.

Yet some students of the missile crisis have gone too far, raising a counterfactual argument to claim that the CIA's misestimates were the most significant shortcoming, and that the photo gap, in essence, did not even matter. "Discovery [of the missiles] a week or two earlier in October . . . . would not have changed the situation faced by the president and his advisers," Raymond Garthoff, one of the most esteemed scholars of the crisis, has written.[86] This is probably not the most appropriate counterfactual argument to pose, given that the missiles were found none too soon. A more significant question is: What would have happened if the missiles had been found even slightly later?

If some combination of the administration's caution, more active Soviet radars, mechanical problems with the aircraft or cameras, or inclement weather had delayed discovery by as lit-

tle as a week to 10 days, then the first sighting would have correlated with a judgment that some SSMs were already capable of being launched, with who knows what consequences for ExComm's deliberations.[87] It was the administration's restraint in the face of a blatant Soviet deception/provocation that won allied and world opinion over to the US position very quickly. That restraint might have been even more sorely tested than it was if some missiles, when discovered, were simultaneously deemed operational. Then, too, the looming mid-term election helped define what the administration saw as its window of opportunity for a negotiated settlement.[88] Appreciably shortening the amount of

---

[83] George termed the Intelligence Community's performance a "near-failure" of the "first magnitude" in *Deterrence,* 473. See also Gil Merom, "The 1962 Cuban Intelligence Estimate," *Intelligence and National* Security 14, no. 3 (Autumn 1999): 52. The pre-14 October intelligence product was "deficient due to *operational,* as much as *analytical,* reasons," according to Merom.
[84] Bundy, *Danger,* 420.

[85] Raymond Garthoff, "US Intelligence in the Cuban Missile Crisis," 53–55; James Wirtz, "Organizing for Crisis Intelligence," 139, 142–45; James Blight and David Welch, "The Cuban Missile Crisis and Intelligence Performance," 199— all in *Intelligence and National Security* 13, no. 3 (Autumn 1998).
[86] Garthoff, "US Intelligence," 24.

[87] "I am sure the impact on American thinking would have been shattering if we had not detected the missiles before they were deployed . . . ," former Deputy Director for Intelligence Ray Cline later observed. "Commentary: The Cuban Missile Crisis," *Foreign Affairs* 68, no. 4 (Fall 1989): 194. By 20 October, the CIA was estimating that the San Cristóbal SSM site, the most advanced of several under construction, "could now have full operational readiness." McAuliffe, ed., *CIA Documents,* 228. The five days of deliberations in the interim were vital in helping the president achieve his preference for a limited objective, i.e., the removal of offensive weapons rather than an invasion of Cuba. Sheldon Stern, *Averting the "Final Failure"* (Stanford, CA: Stanford University Press, 2003), 132–37.
[88] Though the election largely went unmentioned during ExComm's deliberations, at one critical juncture, a Republican (later identified as Treasury Secretary C. Douglas Dillon) passed a frank note to presidential speechwriter Ted Sorensen: "Have you considered the very real possibility that if we allow Cuba to complete installation and operational readiness of missile bases, the next House of Representatives is likely to have a Republican majority?" Theodore Sorensen, *Kennedy* (New York: Harper & Row, 1965), 688.

> ## "
> **Kennedy faced the prospect of explaining why they had degraded the only intelligence-gathering tool that was indispensable.**
> ## "

time left before the 6 November voting suggests that the missile crisis might have played out very differently. Assuming that President Kennedy's determination to avoid an armed conflict remained fixed, he might have had to settle the crisis on less advantageous terms, such as an explicit exchange of Soviet offensive weapons in Cuba for the Jupiter missiles in Turkey.[89]

What actually happened, of course, matters more than what might have been. Yet by that measure, too, the photo gap was more significant than the consistently wrong estimates. The failure to anticipate Khrushchev's gamble, to be sure, was a serious mistake that warranted *ex post facto* study.[90] But was the emphasis on this inability to predict the future justified when the far more critical issue was intelligence collection—or, more accurately, the lack thereof? As one scholar of the analytical process has perceptively written, it really should not have mattered "what intelligence 'thought'" about the likelihood of missiles being introduced into Cuba. "But it did matter, impera-

tively, that intelligence collect the data which would permit a firm judgment whether or not the missiles were there."[91]

Political Cover-up

It is indisputable, in any event, that the photo gap far exceeded the misestimates as a genuine political problem for the administration. Once the formerly villainous U-2 had been transformed, virtually overnight, into a heroic tool, it was more than awkward for the administration to admit that the CIA, in Helms's words, had been "enjoined to stay well away from what we called the business [western] end of the island."[92] Although no one inside the executive branch had been exactly complacent, President Kennedy faced the uncomfortable prospect of

explaining why his administration had degraded the only intelligence-gathering tool that was indispensable until it was almost too late.[93] The photo gap also left the president vulnerable to charges, reasonable or otherwise, that he had been taken in by the Soviets' elaborate deception, to a point where the administration had even tried to foist a false sense of security onto the country.[94]

Well before a settlement of the crisis, ExComm members discussed how to create the widespread impression in public that the administration had been as vigilant as advertised, and that the missiles had been discovered at the earliest reasonable moment.[95] Deflecting congres-

---

[89] The president was prepared to authorize the so-called "Cordier ploy," if direct negotiations failed to produce a settlement. This scheme envisioned a public *quid pro quo* ostensibly proposed by the UN secretary general. Eric Pace, "Rusk Tells a Kennedy Secret: Fallback Plan in Cuba Crisis," *New York Times*, 28 August 1987.

[90] At the same time, the influence of National Intelligence Estimates can be overrated. Policymakers tend to embrace estimates that "validate their own certainties," as one leading scholar has noted. Harold Ford, *CIA and the Vietnam Policymakers* (Washington: CIA Center for the Study of Intelligence, 1998), 12.

[91] Cynthia Grabo, *Anticipating Surprise* (Lanham, MD: University Press of America, 2004), 140.

[92] Helms, *Shoulder*, 212. Gen. Maxwell Taylor seems to have been the only ExComm member whose memoir explicitly referred to the administration's problem vis-à-vis the photo gap. He absolved the president of responsibility and placed the onus on the CIA. "My impression is that the President was never made fully aware of these limitations on our primary source of information, mainly because the intelligence community did not bring the situation forcibly to his attention and urge approval of low-level reconnaissance when the U-2s could not fly." Maxwell Taylor, *Swords and Ploughshares* (New York: Norton, 1972), 263.

[93] The State Department was certainly uncomfortable about its role. In March 1963, for example, Deputy Under Secretary U. Alexis Johnson, in response to a CIA memo reconstructing the attenuation of U-2 overflights, defensively asserted that no useful purpose would be served by recording the "various positions taken by the various individuals or institutions concerned." Memorandum for McCone, "U-2 Overflights of Cuba, 29 August through 14 October 1962," 6 March 1963, Document 626, microfiche supplement to *FRUSvIX*.

[94] William Taubman, *Khrushchev* (New York: Norton, 2003), 557. Reflecting criticism that might have become widespread, one conservative critic asked what the American public should think about a president "who, in the 59th year of the Communist enterprise, is shocked when a Communist lies to him?" James Burnham, "Intelligence on Cuba," *National Review*, 20 November 1962. In his posthumously published memoir, Robert Kennedy admitted that "We had been deceived by Khrushchev, but we had also fooled ourselves." The next sentence, however, claimed that "No official within the government had ever suggested to President Kennedy that the Russian buildup in Cuba would include missiles." Robert Kennedy, *Thirteen Days* (New York: Norton, 1969), 27–28.

sional curiosity, not to mention skeptics in the media, promised to be a very delicate problem. On 5 September, acting DCI Carter had informed senators on the Foreign Relations and Armed Services Committees that the CIA was in no way "assuming" that SSMs would not be implanted in Cuba.[96] On 17 September, before the same committees, Rusk gave similar assurances about the administration's vigilance and the quality of intelligence being gathered. "[With respect to missile sites] we do have very firm information indeed, and of a most reliable sort," the secretary of state testified, seven days after he had helped to attenuate that reliable coverage.[97]

As it turned out, propagating the notion that the missiles had been discovered at the earliest reason-

> **"**
>
> **McCone's prescience did not win him admission into the president's inner circle.**
>
> **"**

able opportunity received an ironic assist from Kenneth Keating, the president's congressional nemesis. The New York senator, as evinced by his 10 October floor statement, seemed to have discovered the missiles several days before the administration. The media's subsequent fixation over Keating's supposedly superior intelligence tended to obfuscate the genuine issue in the weeks leading up to 14 October. The photo gap, in other words, was obscured by a controversy—Keating's ostensible "scoop"—that was truly a red herring.[98]

The last aspect of the photo gap that merits comment is the effect the secret had on the all-important relationship between the nation's chief intelligence officer and the president—actually, both Kennedys, in this case. McCone's prescience did not win him admission into the president's innermost circle of advisers.[99] It had the opposite effect. The DCI became mightily resented, not

only for having been right—which he was not inclined to let anyone forget for a moment—but also for being privy to an embarrassing truth.[100] Ultimately, McCone's loyalty and ambition (like others, he fancied himself a successor to Rusk) were such that the DCI went along with the fiction, in congressional testimony and elsewhere, that the missiles had been found as early as reasonably possible.[101] Yet that scarcely mattered. The Kennedys now distrusted their DCI more than ever, as revealed by their private conversation on 4 March regarding a Marquis Childs column on the photo gap.[102] Although the column did not actually contradict the administration's public position, the mere fact that someone

---

[95] Robert Kennedy, as might be expected, raised this thorny question on 22 October and promptly tried to forge a quick consensus, namely, that surveillance flights would not have "been able to tell up until the last ten days or two weeks." Stern, *"Final Failure,"* 143–44, 152–53.

[96] US Senate, *Executive Sessions of the Senate Foreign Relations Committee Together with Joint Sessions with the Senate Armed Services Committee*, vol. XIV, 87th cong., 2nd sess., (Washington: Government Printing Office, 1986), 689, 716.

[97] Ibid., 760, 765. Present at both of these closed hearings was Richard B. Russell (D-Georgia), whose memory for tiny but critical facts was legendary. Typically, one of the first questions Russell shrewdly asked McCone when congressional leaders were finally briefed about the SSMs on 22 October was whether the SAMs were operational. "I'm sure you're monitoring this [electronic emissions]," said Russell, before McCone informed him that SAM radars "have been latching onto our U-2s the last couple of days." Stern, *"Final Failure,"* 161–62.

---

[98] Another red herring was the speculation in the media (and rumor on Capitol Hill) that the administration allegedly knew before Keating but withheld the information so as to maximize the electoral gain from a showdown with Moscow. Finally, the misestimates, which became public knowledge almost immediately, also drew attention away from the near-failure to collect intelligence.

---

[99] A measure of this fact was that McCone was deliberately kept in the dark about the secret *quid pro quo*, despite openly advocating a public trade of the Jupiter missiles during ExComm meetings. McCone's exclusion here, however, may have had more to do with the DCI's relationship with Dwight Eisenhower and other Republicans. Since Kennedy intended to disinform the former president about the true parameters of the settlement (and did), telling McCone the truth was impossible. Stern, *"Final Failure,"* 388.

[100] In addition, McCone's continued hard line on Cuba and some bruising clashes with Defense Secretary McNamara over the Soviet withdrawal caused some teeth-gnashing within an administration trying hard to get the subject of Cuba off the front pages in early 1963. Guthman and Shulman, eds., *Robert Kennedy*, 14.

[101] If photos had been taken earlier than mid-October, McCone testified, they probably would not have been sufficiently definitive. *FRUSvIX*, 714. Robert Kennedy recalled that "I used to see him [McCone] all the time then [in early 1963] . . . so that we wouldn't have the whole thing bust wide open." Robert Kennedy Oral History, 30 April 1964, JFKL, 224.

[102] Marquis Childs, "Blank Spot in Cuban Picture," *Washington Post*, 4 March 1963.

> ## "
> ### Telling the president and his top advisers what they prefer not to believe . . . is not a job for the faint of heart.
> ## "

other than the White House was obviously putting out a version of what happened, and thus keeping the issue alive, incensed the Kennedys. According to Robert Kennedy, Childs was claiming that the CIA was putting out information against the administration, trying to make itself look good. "Yeah," the president acidly remarked, " . . . he's a real bastard, that John McCone." "Well, he was useful at [one] time," the attorney general observed. "Yeah, but boy, it's really evaporate[d]," responded the president. ". . . Everybody's onto him now."[103]

In Conclusion

Apart from clarifying key dynamics on the eve of the missile crisis, the photo gap is interesting because it speaks to issues of

moment today, not the least of which is the difficulty of being the nation's chief intelligence officer and the qualities that make for an effective one. Telling the president and his top advisers what they prefer not to believe, or advocating a risk they want to avoid, is not a job for the faint of heart. The story of the photo gap is a reminder that the success or failure of the Intelligence Community unavoidably depends on the human factor: the character and capacities of the men and women in critical positions, along with the nature of relationships at the very top.

In January 1969, during his farewell address as director of the State Department's Bureau of Intelligence and Research, Thomas Hughes, remarked: "Over the long run, the prospect for preserving intelligence and policy in their most constructive orthodox roles will depend on the real-life resistance which intelligence officers

apply to these pressures [from policymakers], as well as to the self-imposed restraints which impede the policymakers from originally exerting them."[104]

Hughes's observation was offered after eight years of firsthand exposure to the often troubled relationship between the Intelligence Community and the Kennedy/Johnson administrations during the fateful 1960s, which included McCone's entire tenure as DCI. The run-up to the missile crisis may not represent the model behavior Hughes had in mind, but, decades later, the government seems as far removed as ever from his prescription. Judging from such episodes as policymakers' failure to act against al-Qa'ida in the 1990s and the misappropriation of flawed estimates about Iraq in 2002, at critical junctures US policymakers still receive and absorb the intelligence they prefer rather than need. The recent establishment of a director of national intelligence, in and of itself, is not likely to ameliorate this problem.

---

[103] Conversation between J. F. Kennedy and R. F. Kennedy, Item 9A.6, 4 March 1963, Transcript and Recording of Cassette C (side 2), Presidential Recordings, JFKL. Later in the day, and after a conversation between the president and McGeorge Bundy, McCone discussed the photo gap with the president, who said the photo gap was being used to drive a wedge into the administration, one that would pit the CIA against the State and Defense Departments. He hoped that McCone could avoid making any statements that would "exacerbate the situation." McCone assured the president that that "would not happen." *FRUSvXI*, 713–14.

---

[104] Thomas Hughes, *The Fate of Facts in a World of Men* (New York: Foreign Policy Association, 1976), 27.

Twenty Years of Officers in Residence

John Hollister Hedley

> **"**
>
> **CIA's version of the State Department program has flourished.**
>
> **"**

John Hollister Hedley has served more than three decades with the CIA and helps oversee the Officer-in-Residence Program.

Harry Fitzwater was convinced that he knew a good idea when he saw one. And he regarded the State Department's Ambassador-in-Residence Program as a win-win-win idea: Having an ambassador spend a year between overseas assignments teaching in a university was good for the students and faculty, good for the ambassador, and good for the State Department as an institution. Believing that imitation is the sincerest form of flattery, Fitzwater, then the deputy director for administration at the Central Intelligence Agency, decided that the CIA could run its own version of the State Department program, albeit on a modest scale. His vision has flourished and the program, now in its 20th year, stands as a model for nurturing relations between intelligence and academia.

First Steps

In an August 1985 memorandum to the CIA executive director and his counterparts heading the other Agency directorates, Fitzwater announced an Officer-in-Residence (OIR) Program that would:

Assist Agency staff recruiting efforts by placing in selected schools experienced officers who can spot promising career candidates, can counsel students as to career opportunities, and can use their knowledge and experience to address questions or concerns students may have regarding the Agency.

Encourage the study and knowledge of the intelligence profession through participating in seminars, courses and research.

Afford senior officers a year or two to recharge their intellectual batteries in an academic setting by teaching in an area of academic or work-related expertise.[1]

Fitzwater handpicked one of his senior managers, Harold "Hal" Bean, who was just completing four years as head of the CIA's Office of Training and Education, to pioneer the program. In the fall of 1985, Bean occupied an office at Washington's Georgetown University, famous for its School of Foreign Service. He recalls that Director of Central Intelligence William J. Casey—widely known for his free-wheeling advocacy of "actionable" intelligence and less well known for his interest in scholarship—endorsed the nascent OIR program.[2]

---

[1] Harry E. Fitzwater (Deputy Director for Administration) memorandum, "The Officer-in-Residence Program at Colleges and Universities," 6 August 1985, DD/A Registry 85-2054/6.

All statements of fact, opinion, or analysis expressed in this article are those of the author. Nothing in the article should be construed as asserting or implying US government endorsement of an article's factual statements and interpretations.

> ❝
> ## The lesson about the importance of openness on campus came the hard way.
> ❞

Bean brought a wealth of experience to Fitzwater's experiment. His varied career had included overseas postings in France and Germany, service in the science and technology directorate as executive officer on the Glomar Explorer project, and assignment as chief of support for the Soviet-East European Division in the Directorate of Operations. In addition, he was personable, thoughtful about his new venture on campus, and eager to teach, do research, and meet students and faculty members.

Even so, the fall of 1985 was not a time when one could assume a tension-free beginning to a program that placed a serving CIA officer on a university campus. Faculty members, if not students, were well aware of the backdrop of Vietnam-era protests, the Watergate scandal, the Church Committee investigations of covert action operations, and—at that very time—the CIA's acknowledged role in mining Nicaraguan harbors as part of the Reagan administration's mounting support for the "contras" fighting to overthrow Nicaragua's leftist Sandinista government.

The Importance of Not Being "Spooky"

A lesson learned at the outset of the OIR program was the importance of openness. Bean credits

---

2 Interview with Harold Bean, 23 June 2005, Herndon, VA.

his acceptance by Georgetown faculty, students, and administration to his openness about who he was and why he was there: to teach and do research as a member of the academic "team." The day he arrived on campus, Bean hung on the walls of his office an armload of framed CIA memorabilia and awards bearing the seal and name of the Agency, clearly indicating his affiliation. He is convinced that students and faculty appreciated the fact that he was not being "spooky."

The lesson came the hard way to another pioneer, for the success of the first OIR on the east coast was immediately followed by a disaster on the west coast. Although records are lacking, anecdotal indicators suggest that George Chritton, the first operations officer to be an OIR, felt constrained in what he could or should say and how visible and communicative he should be

The first OIR, Hal Bean (left), compares notes with one of the latest, Paul Frandano, at Georgetown University.

when he went to the University of California at Santa Barbara in the fall of 1987. Whether or not his "no comments" and refusals to talk about subjects were excessive, he apparently felt that he had to minimize exposure and say very little. Anti-Agency demonstrators seized the opportunity to stage a protest that led to numerous arrests and the kind of flare-up that a host university and the Agency equally wish to avoid. Chritton's arrival was handicapped by the fact that the administrator who had approved having an OIR at UC/Santa Barbara had left at the end of the previous academic year and been replaced by someone who knew nothing about it. Whether the OIR's mission was not clear, the perception of a recruitment objective was not adequately addressed, or it was a case of bad chemistry, the fact is that Chritton's arrival inspired suspicion rather than confidence. Chritton quickly left.

That same year, however, James T. McInnis took a page from Bean's book when he became an OIR at the Lyndon Baines Johnson School of Public Affairs of the University of Texas/Austin. In an interview with a campus newspaper, he made no bones about the contrast between his arrival and Chritton's, telling his interviewer that "I'm not a spook. I come out of the Directorate of Administration . . . so [Chritton's] kind of creeping in there [at Santa Barbara] clandestinely . . . was probably a mistake. He should have done it more openly and announced."[3]

McInnis noted how in his first week, through interviews with the student *Daily Texan* and the LBJ school publication, "we did some things right up front and kind of let them know that I'm here." He paid attention to concerns about possible recruiting efforts and minced no words in going on record that "I'm not a recruiter. What I'm doing here is educating people."[4]

McInnis benefited from the unequivocal public backing of Max Sherman, dean of the LBJ School, who told the student newspaper, "There is nothing covert [about the OIR program]. . . . McInnis will be identified as a CIA agent, and he will be available to work with people. It's a very straightforward program . . . . People should understand how the CIA operates, because it is a major federal agency with a great deal of influence."[5]

Also in fall of 1987, Noel Firth succeeded Bean at Georgetown; then, in the fall of 1988, Laurie Kurtzweg, an analyst of Soviet economics in the CIA's Directorate of Intelligence began teaching as an OIR in George Washington University's School of Public and International Affairs. Both followed the example of Bean and McInnis: They succeeded by being models of openness, welcoming campus newspaper interviews, and mak-

> **"**
> **Concern that an officer might recruit students was a show-stopper for some would-be hosts.**
> **"**

ing clear that they were not on campus to recruit.

At George Washington, Kurtzweg's arrival sparked a lively exchange of editorial opinions and letters-to-the-editor in the campus newspaper. But even a student editorial writer critical of the Agency acknowledged that "Dr. Kurtzweg was forthright on her role with the CIA and the program itself. From what I have seen, Dr. Kurtzweg seems to be an excellent teacher and unquestionably an expert in her field."[6] In addition to teaching a course on the political economy of Soviet reforms, Kurtzweg gave lectures in other courses and for campus groups, as OIRs are encouraged to do.

Sensitivity over Recruitment

A concern raised on virtually every campus—and a show-stopper for some would-be hosts—was the prospect that an officer would exploit access to students and faculty by spotting and assessing potential recruits. The reality that the pioneers faced on their campuses made clear that this was a highly sensitive issue. In fact, Fitzwater's internal

memorandum launching the program did envision a recruitment role for OIRs—they could and should, *when asked*, "counsel students as to career opportunities" and "use their knowledge and experience to address questions or concerns students may have regarding the Agency," as Fitzwater put it, but the student would be the one to take the initiative.[7] Farther into his initial memorandum, Fitzwater reiterated that the OIR program would "assist Agency staff recruiting efforts," but he put it into a benign perspective: "As pointed out above, it is our desire that in addition to teaching and engaging in research relevant to Agency interests these officers will serve as role models—prompting the students with whom they associate to consider a career in intelligence."[8] Serving as a role model best describes what experience indicates to be as close as an OIR should come to recruitment. Assurances about this thus became the first order of business in the dialogue with prospective host universities and with students and faculty when an OIR arrived on campus.

The current Agency regulation governing the OIR program no longer even mentions recruitment as a goal. That subject is touched upon only by saying that the program "provides qualified Agency employees with the opportunity to further the mission of the Agency by . . .

[3] *Images*, University of Texas campus newspaper, 29 April 1988: 9–10.
[4] Ibid.
[5] *Daily Texan*, 2 November 1987: 1.

[6] Chris McGinn, "The CIA on campus: The debate is far from over," *GW Hatchet*, 6 October 1988: 5.

[7] Fitzwater.
[8] Ibid.

> ❝
> **Boston and Georgetown made possible the first OIR courses devoted strictly to intelligence.**
> ❞

responding to questions students and faculty may have about the Agency and the intelligence profession."[9] Memoranda of agreement exchanged with prospective host universities clearly state that, as a term of the assignment, "The OIR may respond freely to students' questions about life as a professional intelligence officer. *OIR's are expressly prohibited, however, from actively recruiting university students or any other individuals for professional employment with, or service to, the CIA.* Individuals expressing interest in a career at CIA will be referred to the Agency's public Web site or to appropriate recruitment components for assistance."[10]

In practice, university students—including those not enrolled in an OIR's class—do seek out answers to questions about career possibilities and OIRs are expected to respond helpfully. As the author knows from his own OIR experience at Georgetown, administrators and other faculty will suggest that a student talk with the OIR, who is looked upon as the resident expert on a prospective intelligence career. The student "walk-ins" who seek out the OIR (often—certainly at Georgetown—already set on the idea of a career in foreign service) usually are curious about just what it is that one would or could do at the CIA.

---

[9] Agency Regulation 20-57, "Officer in Residence Program," 3 November 1997.

[10] Memorandum of Understanding, "The Officer-in-Residence Program," unpublished document of the CIA's Center for the Study of Intelligence, September 2005. Italics appear in the original.

Some students also raise concerns about getting into the CIA—none handled more deftly than a situation the late Floyd Paseman encountered as OIR at Marquette University. A student came to his office and, after some hemming and hawing, said he was worried about taking a polygraph test, which he understood the CIA required as part of the hiring process. Paseman kindly assured him that the Agency understood we were all young once, that growing up sometimes involved doing things we would not want our parents to know about, and that the Agency accepted this as part of what makes us individuals. As long as he was truthful and not hiding something serious, such as a felony, he would not be ruled out. Turning red, the student told Paseman he was under probation after being caught streaking naked across the basketball court during one of Marquette's games. Managing not to laugh aloud, Paseman assured him that, unless he had been a frequent streaker, this alone was not likely to disqualify him![11]

---

[11] Floyd Paseman, *A Spy's Journey: A CIA Memoir* (St. Paul, MN: Zenith Press, 2004), 210.

Teaching Intelligence

During the program's early years, OIRs taught intelligence-related courses based on their expertise. In Bean's first semester at Georgetown, for example, he taught a graduate course on management problems in foreign affairs, including those common to Intelligence Community organizations. Noting Bean's research for Georgetown's Institute for the Study of Diplomacy on the effect of terrorism on diplomacy, Dean Peter Krogh asked him to offer an undergraduate course on the subject. So Bean also taught "Diplomacy and Terrorism," and published a booklet on the subject. At Texas, McInnis offered a course on Mexico and also taught about international terrorism. Kurtzweg taught Soviet economics; Firth offered "Analysis and Forecasting for International Affairs"; and other OIRs lectured on government and politics in the Middle East or Latin America.

Two especially hospitable academic settings—Boston University and Georgetown—made possible the first running of courses devoted strictly to intelligence. When Arthur Hulnick arrived in Boston in 1989, a survey course on intelligence already was being offered by a professor who was a navy reservist Hulnick knew and had helped with suggestions about the course. "Why don't you teach it?" Hulnick was asked, "You're the expert."[12] Hulnick agreed and began for Boston University what would become perhaps the best curriculum of intelligence courses in the United States. At Georgetown, in the spring of 1994, I taught a course purely on intelligence, entitled "CIA and the Changing Role of US Intelligence."

By the end of its first decade, the OIR program's focus on all campuses was on teaching intelligence, a substantive mission transcending the teaching of related subjects, plus guest lectures, student conferences, and the like. Teaching about intelligence was facilitated by the arrival of several reputable books that could be adopted as texts or assigned as required reading in what had previously been a slim selection.[13]

Newly selected OIRs are given an opportunity to develop a syllabus on their own for the intelligence course they will teach. They receive no script or "party line," although resources are available through the CIA's Center for the

> ❝
> **OIRs develop their own syllabi . . . there is no 'party line.'**
> ❞

Study of Intelligence (CSI).[14] New and continuing OIR's attend an early summer seminar on the teaching of intelligence taught by former OIRs. This facilitates the sharing of lessons learned about adjusting to academe. The seminar's focus is substantive but not prescriptive. Potential textbook choices and related books are discussed. Practical questions—such as how to craft a syllabus; how much reading to expect of students; and how to go about assigning papers, giving tests, organizing lectures, and doing research—are answered. Although a household move absorbs time and energy over the summer, most OIRs find time to read, utilize reference materials, and prepare for the fall semester.

Each course must be academically sound, enrich the university's curriculum, and pass muster with the university department hosting the OIR. Generally, OIRs are expected to survey the structure, functions, and challenges of national intelligence, including collection, analysis, support to policy, and issues

of accountability, politicization, oversight, and ethics. Their focus is not on tradecraft, but on the way the intelligence process works and the issues and challenges it involves. Their value-added is the insiders' perspective.

OIRs may offer additional courses as appropriate to their career backgrounds and the universities' requirements. They are encouraged to participate fully in the academic life of the university, doing research and writing and participating in informal seminars and workshops. But the core mission is to provide a window into the CIA that will help illuminate for students and the broader university community the role of intelligence in US foreign policy and national security and its place in a free society.

Selecting OIRs

Determining who becomes an OIR is a process that evolved unevenly following Fitzwater's initial informal appeal to his fellow deputy directors to offer candidates. From the beginning, OIRs have been dependent on their home component to pay their salaries, in absentia, and to cover related expenses, such as for books, travel, and household moves. Because of this decentralized funding, in the early years selection essentially was left to the home components. From time to time this doubtless involved irregular and informal arrangements struck between individual officers, their home office or directorate, and an interested

---

12 Arthur Hulnick, telephone conversation with the author, 6 August 2005.
13 A useful basic text was Berkowitz and Goodman's *Strategic Intelligence for American National Security* (Princeton, NJ: University Press, 1989). Supplementing that was Abram Shulsky's *Silent Warfare,* 2nd ed., (Washington, DC: Brassey's, 1993). Then, Loch Johnson updated his *America's Secret Power: The CIA in a Democratic Society* (Oxford, UK: University Press, 1989) with *Secret Agencies: US Intelligence in a Hostile World* (New Haven, CT: Yale University Press, 1996). British authors helped considerably, with Christopher Andrew's brilliant *For the President's Eyes Only: Secret Intelligence and the American Presidency from Washington to Bush* (New York: Harper Collins, 1995), followed by Michael Herman's *Intelligence Power in Peace and War* (Oxford, UK: University Press, 1996).

14 The Center for the Study of Intelligence is a small research unit that promotes broader understanding of the history of intelligence and lessons learned from its practice. In addition to overseeing the OIR program, it incorporates the CIA history staff; publishes the quarterly journal, *Studies in Intelligence*; and manages the CIA Exhibit Center. The Center runs conferences and sponsors the writing of intelligence monographs.

---

host institution—perhaps one where the would-be OIR had a friend on the faculty. Once on campus, the OIRs' academic involvement in the early years of the program varied widely. One spent his time pursuing a master's degree in computational linguistics while acting as a teaching assistant in the mathematics department. Others have taught physical geology, electrical engineering, and psychology.[15]

After the program's first decade, an audit by the CIA Inspector General concluded that the program was "overdue for an Agency regulation to ensure standardization in the program's operation and administration of individual OIR assignments." It called for CSI to play a more active role in defining the mission of the OIRs and selecting host institutions, in part to discourage use of the program to accommodate employees' personal preferences.[16]

As a result, since the mid-1990s, the OIR selection process has been more centrally handled, although funding remains decentralized. CSI meets with component administrative officers in October each year to review a timeline for the process and the list of universities seeking OIRs. The program is advertised during the fall, including through internal media and routine

---

[15] "Report of Audit: Administration of the Intelligence Officer-in-Residence Program," Office of Inspector General, Central Intelligence Agency, 12 March 1996, 4–6.
[16] Ibid., 12.

> **"**
> ## In contrast to the selection process, funding remains decentralized.
> **"**

vacancy notices. The job description notes that a Ph.D., while highly desirable, is not mandatory, but applicants must have a master's degree, broad experience in intelligence, research capabilities, and strong interpersonal skills. Prior teaching experience is an advantage. Interested officers must supply supporting documentation along with their application.

The application packages go to the candidate's home component, which determines the maximum number of OIR positions it is prepared to fund. Applicants are screened, and the names of those approved for assignment—if selected—are forwarded to CSI for final review. CSI then performs its own evaluations of the candidates, which include interviews, and matches its choices to the number of positions each component will fund. Successful nominees are notified early in the new year. Matching candidates to universities takes into account the preferences of both the individuals and the universities, a process that sometimes involves campus visits, arranged by CSI. The goal is to confirm assignments by March, so that the new OIRs can bring their current assignments to a close in time for the annual CSI seminar in June for those heading out to campuses the following fall.

Choosing Universities

There is no rigid formula for selecting host universities, but CSI—through campus visits, phone calls, and correspondence with universities seeking OIRs—looks for a strong academic foundation in fields related to intelligence, whether international studies, public policy, political science, or history. Ideally, CSI seeks programs near the "take-off' stage with respect to intelligence studies, where the presence of an OIR could make a major difference. Students at Washington, DC-area universities typically have innumerable opportunities to be exposed to intelligence studies and already have a virtual conveyer belt of guest lecturers and current or retired CIA officers as adjunct faculty. The program's aim is to extend the program well beyond Washington's capital beltway. And, to spread the impact of limited resources farther, CSI prefers not to focus year after year on the same universities.

The OIR program has remained small, with rarely as many as a dozen officers in place in a given year. More universities seek OIRs than there are officers to fill them. For the fall of 2005, 10 universities were listed as potential host institutions, but only three were chosen by successful OIR applicants: Georgetown (the only university to have continuous representation), The University of Miami, and the University of Georgia. The three new OIRs join seven others completing their tours—at Arizona, Georgia

---

> ## "Nervous department chairmen can be challenges."

Tech, Indiana, John Jay College of Criminal Justice, Kentucky, MIT, and Texas A&M—bringing the total number of officers currently in the field to 10. Even though the scope of the program remains modest after two decades, 100 CIA officers have been posted to 51 institutions as widely scattered as Harvard, Princeton, Stanford, Oklahoma, Virginia, Dartmouth, and Southern California.[17]

Faculty Hurdles

Although student response to OIRs in recent years has been invariably positive, overcoming faculty skeptics—and nervous department chairmen anxious about adverse faculty reaction—continues to be a common challenge. Negative faculty attitudes, which usually involve a small minority, tend to arise from major misconceptions and misplaced concerns. A classic example is the experience of Brian Gilley, who arrived as the first OIR at Duke University only to discover that, although he was welcome to teach courses in the Department of Economics—his

field—the Department of Political Science and Public Policy balked at offering an undergraduate survey course on intelligence on the grounds that "Duke students wouldn't like a course like that."[18] Biding his time, Gilley proceeded to teach intelligence-related graduate courses on macroeconomic modeling and senior seminars dealing with economic growth and development theory as applied to Eastern Europe and East Asia. Student reviews were outstanding—the response was so effusive that, for Gilley's second year, the economics and political science department chairmen found that they were able, after all, to accommodate Gilley's teaching in both departments. The result was an intelligence course that was so oversubscribed that another section was added. And the chairmen of both departments appealed to the CIA to allow Gilley to stay another year in order to give the maximum number of Duke undergraduates the opportunity to take the intelligence course.

More recently, Robert Vickers arrived as the first OIR at the Massachusetts Institute of Technology at the invitation of the Security Studies Program, only

to discover dissenting voices in the Political Science Department, questioning his lack of university teaching experience. (Although some universities want OIRs with Ph.Ds and teaching experience, most recognize—as did MIT's Security Studies Program—that a senior CIA officer can bring unique experience to the classroom that is an acceptable substitute.) In Vickers's case, a team-teaching arrangement was worked out. Security Studies Program Director Harvey M. Sapolsky explained that "it was difficult to gain agreement within the Political Science Department to allow Bob to teach," and the team approach—involving Sapolsky, a political science professor, and Vickers—"was a way to break down the opposition."[19]

As is usually the case, the classroom experience alone did not carry the day. Due to space shortages, Vickers had his office in the political science building rather than with the Security Studies Program. "This turned out to be fortuitous," Sapolsky explained, "because Bob is very outgoing and soon had many friends where the opposition was based. He was very open in answering questions and participated constructively in many seminars."[20] Vickers now is offering his own undergraduate course. "Although recruiting is not his mission,"

---

[17] Certain of the officers who served in earlier years would no longer be considered to be in OIR positions, which now require teaching intelligence at a full-fledged university. The Federal Executive Institute, for example—a training enterprise of the Office of Personnel Management—and the Joint Military Intelligence College—a Defense Intelligence Agency training organization—would not qualify for OIR assignments as once was the case. OIRs also are no longer assigned to the military academies because of the specialized kind of educational experience they provide to groom military officers.

[18] Brian Gilley, e-mail to the author, 19 August 2003, and conversation with the author in McLean, VA, 10 August 2005.

[19] Letter from Harvey M. Sapolsky to Paul M. Johnson, Director of the Center for the Study of Intelligence, 20 June 2005, quoted with the writer's permission.
[20] Ibid.

Sapolsky added, "I think the courses and his enthusiastic presence will be a big plus for those considering an intelligence career. It was, after all, on the students' initiative that we sought out having an officer-in-residence."[21]

Gauging Success

Individually and almost invariably, former OIRs declare their time on campus to have been among their most satisfying Agency assignments. Paseman, for example, described it as "one of the most rewarding and productive" postings of his 35-year career, noting that "the thirst for information about the CIA and intelligence is enormous."[22] Judging from student responses to OIRs—both in enrollment numbers and in course evaluations—and appeals from deans and department heads to extend an OIR or ensure a replacement, universities highly value the program as well.

Several OIR alumni have gone on to teach as adjunct faculty members—the author, for one. Hal Bean taught as an adjunct at Georgetown for 13 years after his OIR tour. George Fidas continues as a prized adjunct faculty member after serving as OIR at George Washington University, as does Lee Strickland at the University of Maryland, and as did Robert Pringle for

---

[21] Ibid.
[22] Paseman, 213.

> ❝
> **Universities throughout the country are seeking to add intelligence courses.**
> ❞

several years at the University of Kentucky. James Olson retired to become a full-time faculty member at Texas A&M, where he had served as an OIR. Michael Turner chose teaching over the CIA for a full-time career, leaving the Agency after an OIR assignment; he now occupies an endowed chair as professor of international relations at Alliant International University in San Diego, where he also teaches at the University of San Diego.

No former OIR has gone farther with a serious academic experience, however, than Arthur Hulnick. Becoming a full-time faculty member was "the last thing I had in mind," Hulnick insists, when he went to Boston University in the fall of 1989. He expected to spend two years as an OIR and then move to a job in recruiting. When the person he hoped to succeed did not leave after two years, Hulnick stayed on in Boston.

As luck would have it, the recruiting office closed at the end of that year, at which time Hulnick's home office advised him that his slot was needed at headquarters and he should either come back or retire. By then he had hit full stride, teaching four courses—a gradu-

ate seminar, history of intelligence, a comparative treatment of foreign intelligence and security systems, and intelligence in a democratic society—and loving it. With 35 years of service, he retired in place and never looked back. Since then, Boston University has appointed him a full-time associate professor and he teaches seven intelligence courses a year.[23]

Looking Ahead

Students entering universities in the fall of 2005 were born after the OIR program began. Although few will have served in the military, the threat of global terrorism has heightened interest in the field of national security. This interest is widely manifest in college curricula, as universities throughout the country are adding or seeking to add intelligence courses.

Intelligence is arguably more important and a more complicated subject to teach than at any time in the history of the OIR program. The relatively few CIA officers who will next take up this unique assignment, no matter how scattered and small in number, will constitute a continuing commit-

---

[23] Telephone interview with the author, 6 August 2005. Hulnick also has written two books, *Fixing the Spy Machine: Preparing American Intelligence for the Twenty-First Century* (Westport, CT: Praeger, 1999) and *Keeping Us Safe: Secret Intelligence and Homeland Security* (Praeger, 2004).

" CIA's OIR program can serve as a model for broadening the Intelligence Community's academic outreach. "

ment and a relatively inexpensive investment in encouraging understanding and further study in the field of intelligence. Hal Bean says one of the things that is most rewarding for him is that, two decades after his time at Georgetown, he sees people at CIA today, not whom he recruited, but who were "tuned in" by the exposure he made possible.[24]

As of this writing, at least a dozen universities are hoping to host a CIA OIR when the

program begins its third decade in the fall of 2006. CIA's experience with its OIR program can serve as a model to share with its partner organizations as they explore ways to broaden the Intelligence Community's future academic outreach.

---

[24] Bean interview.

A Critical Look at Britain's Spy Machinery

Philip H. J. Davies

> **The understated reaction in the UK to [Iraq WMD intelligence failures] has been the source of some curiosity amongst American observers.**

Editor's Note: British political scientist Philip Davies' examination of UK intelligence reporting and analysis prior to Operation Iraqi Freedom in 2003 broadens understanding of US post-mortems on Iraq by setting them in a coalition context. This article is based on seminars that Dr. Davies led at Carleton University's Norman Patterson School of International Affairs and George Washington University's Institute for European and Eurasian Studies in the autumn of 2004, while he was in the United States researching his forthcoming comparative study of UK and US intelligence.[1]

* * *

Requirements Sections are supposed to ensure that goats remain goats.

—Former senior SIS officer.[2]

---

[1] Dr. Davies would like to acknowledge helpful comments from his colleague at the Brunel University Centre for Intelligence and Security Studies, Professor Anthony Glees, and from participants in the Carleton and GW conferences, most notably Prof. Martin Rudner, Prof. Richard Aldrich, and Prof. James Goldgeier. He is also indebted to Michael Herman who, he acknowledges, was probably the first person other than himself to realize that the analysis of Secret Intelligence Service (SIS) structure in Davies' book, *MI6 and the Machinery of Spying* (London: Frank Cass, 2004), had exposed the weakening of Requirements. The research for this article was made possible in part by a Leverhulme Trust Research Fellowship.

Dr. Philip H. J. Davies is deputy director of the Brunel University Centre for Intelligence and Security Studies where he is also senior lecturer in politics. He is the author or co-author of several books on intelligence matters.

Since the invasion of Iraq, the understated reaction in the UK to what one former British official has described as the "worst intelligence failure since 1945" has been the source of some surprise and curiosity amongst American observers of the intelligence process.[3] In the United States, the Intelligence Community, Congress, and commentators alike have been swept up in the intelligence reform debate that culminated in the last-minute passage of the Intelligence Reform and Terrorism Prevention Act in the closing days of the 108th Congress. In Britain there have been a succession of furors to be sure, but these have been only minimally concerned with the actual *failure of intelligence* to discern the limited extent of Iraq's nonconventional weapons programs and capabilities.

For the most part, UK debate has pivoted around three issues: the publication of national assessments of Iraqi capability under the acknowledged authorship of the Joint Intelligence Committee (JIC); the possibility that the government pressured the JIC drafting team to include intelligence reports or claims known or

---

[2] Interview with former senior SIS officer, 27 February 1997.
[3] Information under the Chatham House rule.

---

suspected to be unsound or unreliable; and how the debate about this latter possibility led ultimately to the suicide of Dr. David Kelly in July 2002.[4]

An intensive review of intelligence on so-called "weapons of mass destruction" (WMD) led by Lord Butler of Brockwell (a former Cabinet Secretary) was published in the summer of 2004;[5] however, it attracted far less interest—and far less informed or, at least, comprehending discussion—than the January report of Lord Hutton of Bresagh on the Kelly suicide.[6] Above all, the publication of the Butler review was not heralded with the kind of demands for comprehensive review and reform that accompanied the US Senate Select Committee's report on pre-war intelligence estimates on Iraq.[7]

This may have been a consequence of both the scope of the Butler review and the language of its final report. Butler was tasked to review all major counterproliferation investigations, not just Iraq.[8] As a result, the

> **Analysis is generally the least appreciated aspect of the intelligence process.**

failure on Iraq was examined alongside at least four other, loosely comparable problems—Libya, Iran, North Korea, and the Pakistan-based, transnational Abdul Qadir Khan network—which had been handled successfully. In this context, the Iraq failure was not seen as a comprehensive breakdown of the intelligence process and systemic malaise, but rather as one failure against four successes. Hence, it was viewed as a failure due to Iraq-specific factors that somehow tripped up an otherwise effective system.

The language of the Butler report was likewise comparatively understated. It avoided the often hectoring and accusatory tone of the Senate Select Committee report on US prewar intelligence on Iraq, stayed away from personalizing blame, and examined the Iraq failure chiefly in terms of the "collective responsibility" ethos of Britain's Cabinet government and the collegiality of the JIC system in its Cabinet Office. But it also has to be said that intelligence analysis (or *assessment*, in UK parlance) is gener-

ally the least appreciated and least addressed aspect of the intelligence process in the UK. On the one hand, this is because assessment is scholarly rather than sexy; on the other, as has been pointed out in a number of forums elsewhere, assessment is viewed in the UK as a *government* function and not specifically as an *intelligence* function.[9]

The conclusions reached by Butler's review team were also less hostile than those of the Senate Select Committee. To be sure, they found that a measure of groupthink had been at work—in looking for evidence to corroborate the suspicions that the JIC had insisted on sustaining despite a lack of hard evidence (a long-recognized, inherent risk of the JIC system's collegial methods[10]) and a tendency to overcompensate for the optimistic assessments of the limits of Iraqi nuclear developments discredited after the first Gulf War. But no damning appraisal of comprehensive groupthink, analytical "layering," or "broken corporate culture" appeared in the report. It concluded that publishing intelligence for public persuasion in the so-called September Dos-

[4] See, for example, Anthony Glees and Philip H. J. Davies *Spinning the Spies: Intelligence, Open Government and the Hutton Inquiry* (London: Social Affairs Unit, 2004).

[5] Lord Butler of Brockwell, *Review of Weapons of Mass Destruction* (London: TSO, 2004), HC898 of 2004.

[6] Lord Hutton of Bresagh, *Report of the Inquiry into the Circumstances Surrounding the Death of Dr. David Kelly C.M.G.* (London: TSO, 2004).

[7] Senate Select Committee on Intelligence, *Report on the US Intelligence Community's Prewar Intelligence Assessments on Iraq* (Washington: United States Congress, 2004), S108-301.

[8] This brief parallels that of the Presidential Commission on the Capabilities of the United States Regarding Weapons of Mass Destruction, which reported in March 2005; however, the SSCI report was published at roughly the same time as the Butler review and set the tone and agenda for US intelligence reform discussions in a way that the Presidential Commission has not.

[9] See, for example, Michael Herman *Intelligence Power in Peace and War* (Cambridge: Cambridge University Press, 1996), 265; Philip H. J. Davies, "Ideas of Intelligence: Divergent National Concepts and Institutions," *Harvard International Review* 24, no. 3: 62–64; and "Intelligence Culture and Intelligence Failure in Britain and the United States," *Cambridge Review of International Affairs* 17, no. 3: 496–520.

[10] See, for example, John Hughes Wilson, *Military Intelligence Blunders and Cover-Ups* (London: Robinson, 2004), 260–308, 407–8.

sier (drawn from a classified 9 September 2002 JIC estimate) had been a "bad idea" and "should not be repeated" under any circumstances, but that, for the most part, the causes of failure had been Iraq-specific and not endemic.

This is not to say that no institutional or structural issues were raised in Lord Butler's review of intelligence on WMD. Indeed, toward the end of the report, he expressed a number of concerns regarding the effectiveness of the intelligence validation components of the Secret Intelligence Service's management structure—the "Requirements" side of SIS. One of the factors behind the failure of UK Iraq assessments was the practice of placing "greater weight" upon a number of human intelligence (HUMINT) reports "than they could reasonably bear," in the words of the *Review*.[11] Butler identified a structural weakness in SIS's quality control system embodied in its Requirements machinery. According to the report, confronted with both urgent demands for assessments of Iraqi nonconventional weapons capabilities and limited operational resources as a consequence of post–Cold War "peace dividend" cutbacks during the early 1990s, the Requirements system was not equal to the task of a rigorous evaluation of SIS reporting on Iraq.

> ## " The catastrophic failure over Iraq was not just the result of a *short-term* breakdown in the system. "

As the following analysis will show, the malaise in Requirements that led to the intelligence failure on Iraqi WMD represents an even deeper, longer-term trend in the management of SIS than the Butler review identified. During the 1990s, I undertook a detailed administrative history of the Service, in the process discovering how the Requirements component of SIS had been progressively scaled back over more than two decades.[12] It is in this context that we have to understand the breakdown in validation at SIS in 2002—*the catastrophic failure over Iraq was not just a result of a short-term breakdown beginning in the mid-1990s.*

How the Machine Works

For most of its existence, Britain's Secret Intelligence Service has been centered around a basic organizational architecture in which its "Production" side mounts operations in response to specific demands laid upon it by a tasking, validation, and dissemination apparatus referred to as its "Requirements" side.[13] The Production side is divided regionally under area controllers, who oversee an assortment of operational "P Sections," each of which handles several countries and manages the agency's resident stations abroad. The Requirements side and its "R Sections" task the Production side, validate its product, and disseminate that product to SIS consumers at Whitehall and Downing Street. Prior to the 1980s, Production and Requirements were separate and had approximately equal representation on the SIS Board of Directors.

Requirements officers are roughly analogous to reports officers inside the CIA's Directorate of Operations (DO). Partly because SIS is an operational organization with no analytical function (except as a participant in the collective assessment process in the Cabinet Office Joint Intelligence Committee) and partly because of the peculiar circumstances of history, R Sections traditionally have occupied a far more central role in SIS than do reports officers in the DO.[14]

From an industrial management point of view, Requirements plays a dual role within SIS: It provides marketing (representing the agency to its consumers and vice versa) and quality control (scrutinizing SIS product to see that it

---

[11] Butler, 56.

[12] Davies, *MI6 and the Machinery of Spying*.

[13] The following narrative is summarized from the text of *MI6 and the Machinery of Spying*, with citations given for new sources of information acquired since publication or where there are particular points of contention. For a detailed discussion of Requirements in particular, also see my article, "MI6's Requirements Directorate: Integrating Intelligence into the Machinery of Government," *Public Administration* 78, no. 1 (January 2000).

> ## ''Requirements' was responsible for the annual review of intelligence priorities.''

meets consumers' needs in terms of both relevance and reliability). In industry, combining marketing and quality control in a single body would seem counter-intuitive and potentially a conflict of interest between the priorities of selling a profitable volume (increasing revenues) and ensuring a potentially expensive high standard of output (increasing costs). In intelligence, unlike the commercial world, however, there are natural economies of scale in combining these dissimilar tasks into a common organizational entity.

Evolution of "Requirements"

The Requirements side began life as a cluster of consumer-liaison sections shortly after the First World War. Under this scheme, SIS's largest and most powerful consumers—the War Office, Admiralty, Foreign Office, and, later, Royal Air Force—seconded sections of their own intelligence branches to SIS to lobby for their partisan interests.[15]

During and after the Second World War, however, the composition and function of the Requirements Sections, as they were termed after 1946, began to shift. To start with, the sections dealing with economic and industrial intelligence and with scientific and technological intelligence found themselves representing a range of consumers with common intelligence needs. They were no longer single-customer departments. At the same time, the Foreign Office liaison section began to grow into a minor empire of its own, subdivided along the same geographical lines as the Production side's regional divisions, the Area Controllerates. In all three cases, the sections began to be staffed by internal SIS appointees.

Another shift came as a consequence of the Joint Intelligence Committee moving from the Ministry of Defence to the Cabinet Office, in which capacity it was to "give higher direction to and keep under review the organisation and working of intelligence as a whole at home and overseas . . . ."[16] This mandate included formal responsibility for the "national requirements cycle" in which producers and consumers agreed on intelligence requirements and priorities on an annual basis. Under this new system, the Requirements Sections became responsible for overseeing SIS implementation of tasks under what became the annual National Intelligence Requirements Paper. R Section heads also represented SIS on the various JIC subcommittees (which later became Current Intelligence Groups). Both trends shifted Requirements away from partisan representation to a broader tasking, validation, and dissemination role.

For much of SIS's existence, Requirements constituted a significant part of the management structure. When the headquarters staff in the 1930s numbered "less than twenty officers," perhaps half a dozen were members of the liaison sections.[17] After the Second World War, the Requirements Sections were grouped together in a Directorate of Requirements whose director (D/R) sat on the SIS Board of Directors alongside the Director of Production (D/P).

---

[14] Reports officers are something of a dog that has failed to bark in the history of US intelligence and the CIA. Although they occupy a significant nexus between clandestine service officers and Directorate of Intelligence analysts, they have tended to attract far less attention than either in the literature. Indeed, little more than a dozen documents refer to them in the CIA Records Search Tool holdings at the National Archive in College Park. Significantly, however, at one point they were referred to as Requirements/Reports Officers. One of the few published studies of the reports officer role is W. J. McKee's "The Reports Officer: Issues of Quality," reprinted from *Studies in Intelligence* in H. Bradford Westerfield, ed., *Inside CIA's Private World* (London: Yale University Press, 1995), 108–17.

[15] The official history of British intelligence in the Second World War attributes this scheme to the Secret Service Committees of 1919 and 1921 and calls it the "1921 arrangement." See F. H. Hinsley, et al., *British Intelligence in the Second World War* (London: HMSO, 1979), 17. Alan Judd, however, argues that it should really be credited to Director of Military Intelligence George W. M. MacDonogh, who proposed it in 1917. See Alan Judd *The Quest for C: Mansfield Cumming and the Founding of the Secret Service* (London: HarperCollins, 1999), 392–93.

[16] "Terms of Reference for the Joint Intelligence Committee," JIC (57) 101, 1 October 1957, in CAB 158 30, UK National Archive (formerly the Public Record Office).

[17] Christopher Andrew, *Secret Service* (London: Sceptre, 1987), 487.

Losing Ground

From the mid-1970s onward, however, the institutional position of Requirements began to weaken. SIS Chief Sir Maurice Oldfield reorganized Requirements along geographical lines to match both the Controllerates and the Current Intelligence Groups, which drafted national assessments under the Joint Intelligence Committee. Although essentially redistributing the work of the existing sections, this reform also separated the armed service representatives from the Requirements Directorate—moving them out of the chain of command into an SIS Secretariat under the Chief of Service. This deprived D/R of the weight and authority of having the three armed services and the Ministry of Defence behind him on the Board of Directors.

> ## From the mid-1970s onward, the institutional position of Requirements began to weaken.

The 1970s was a period of national financial retrenchment, and SIS suffered from the cutbacks in funds and personnel as much as any other part of the UK defense and security apparatus. In 1979, under SIS Chief Sir Arthur 'Dickie' Franks, it was concluded that Requirements was too small to warrant being a full Directorate. Production and Requirements were amalgamated under a Director of Production and Requirements (D/PR), with the Requirements Sections being managed by a Deputy Director Requirements (DD/R).[18]

This development coincided with a trend during the second half of the decade toward collocating regional Requirements and Production sections within SIS's main office. The rationale for collocation was to allow tasking and validation functions to be more directly factored into operational management. This development was controversial. One senior officer of the period recalls:

The closer relationship between Requirements and Production began to raise all sorts of questions, especially amongst old-school Requirements officers, about whether this arrangement retained the independence of the Requirements process. On the other hand, this arrangement helped the Requirements Section officers know the agent better, helping with the assessment of the product and increasing alertness to the possibility of fabrication. This is particularly important since the case officer develops something of a partnership with his agent, developing a bond of loyalty. This relationship tends to make sheep out of goats and Requirements Sections are supposed to ensure that goats remain goats.[19]

Although numerically and institutionally diminished, the Requirements mechanism continued to operate reasonably effectively until Permanent Secretary of Defence Sir Michael Quinlan conducted a post–Cold War review of intelligence. As a result of the Quinlan Review and subse-

---

[18] This is also sometimes given as Director, Requirements and Production, or D/RP.
[19] Interview with former senior SIS officer, 27 February 1997.

> ❝
>
> ## In contrast to the United States, the JIC had produced a steady stream of national assessments on Iraq.
>
> ❞

quent cuts to intelligence expenditure as part of the "peace dividend," SIS experienced a 25 percent reduction in staffing and expenditure, part of which took the form of a 40 percent decrease in senior staff. The DD/R was abolished and the R Sections were placed under the direct authority of the area controllers. Under the new arrangement, the area controllers, rather than Requirements officers, came to represent SIS on the Current Intelligence Groups of the JIC's Assessments Staff, marginalizing Requirements further by depriving it of its role in the JIC-SIS relationship.[20] The only remnant of formal independence for Requirements was a Requirements Board, headed by a senior R officer, but without representation on the Board of Directors. Just as collocation seemed relatively nonthreatening to the independence of Requirements in 1979, so subordinating the function to the senior Production managers seemed benign to participants at the time.[21]

This realignment, moreover, appeared to be a natural development in line with the spread of information technology. "Modern communications technology and computers," observed one former officer, "have made it easier for everyone to know the same thing at the same time."[22] In other words, the day had passed when

disseminating intelligence involved officers carrying locked briefcases across St. James's Park. The increased centrality of tasking and dissemination dominated perceptions of this change, both to participants and observers (myself included). *The quality control implications were completely overlooked.*

SIS Iraqi Sources

In contrast to the United States, where the Senate Select Committee was perturbed to find a complete absence of national estimates on Iraq before the 2003 invasion,[23] the JIC had produced a steady stream of national assessments on aspects of the Iraqi problem throughout the decade or so prior to the second Gulf war. Lord Butler's inquiry in 2004 systematically retraced the steps of these assessments, paying particular attention to the basis for the estimates on the Iraqi threat in the final year before the invasion. From the

present perspective, however, the crucial interval was the period following operation DESERT FOX in 1998 and the associated withdrawal of UN inspectors from Iraq. At that point, covert human sources acquired a primacy in the assessment process that they did not have when a substantial body of overt information was available through UN auspices.

Butler reveals in his report that SIS had a stable of six human sources inside Iraq. He describes four of these as "main" sources and two of the four as "dominant sources," producing some two-thirds of all intelligence reports on Iraq that were circulated. He cautions that "volume is not necessarily a measure of influence; even a single [report] can have a significant impact." All four of the main sources were considered reliable prior to the invasion and, in most respects, all four emerged as being generally reliable after the war, but with some significant qualifications.

First source: The first dominant source "reported accurately and authoritatively on some issues" but "on production of stocks of chemical and biological agents, he could only report what he learned from others in his circle of high-level contacts in Baghdad." In other words, the first dominant source may have had direct knowledge of a number of key issues but on nonconventional weapons he was reporting hearsay.

---

[20] Mark Urban, *UK Eyes Alpha: The Inside Story of British Intelligence* (London: Faber & Faber, 1996), 29.

[21] Confidential conversation with former senior SIS officer, 19 January 2005.

[22] Interview with former senior SIS officer, 27 February 1997.

[23] Senate Select Committee on Intelligence, *The Intelligence Community's Pre-War Assessments on Iraq,* 51. Senator Bob Graham—in his book *Intelligence Matters* (New York: Random House, 2004), 179–80—describes his reaction at the time as "shocked" that there had been no Intelligence Community estimate of as major a national security issue as Iraq.

> **Iraq reporting appears to have followed proper practices.**

Second and third sources: The second dominant source likewise was judged overall to be "an established and reliable source" whose reporting "on other subjects had previously been corroborated." However, this second source began to pass information received from one of his contacts who acted as a subsource reporting on chemical and biological programs and intentions. The subsource's reporting served to underpin a number of JIC assessments on Iraqi WMD, even though reports based on his information "properly included a caution about the subsource's links to opposition groups and the possibility that his reports would be affected by that." During the post–war SIS validation exercise, "serious doubts" were raised about the reliability of his reports. As a consequence, the reporting from the second dominant source may have been sound where he was reporting his own knowledge, but the information from his subagent was unsound.

Fourth and fifth sources: The other two main sources continued to be judged as reliable under SIS post–war validation efforts, but, Lord Butler notes significantly, "reports from those sources tended to present a less worrying view of Iraqi chemical and biological weapons capability than [reporting] from the sources whose reporting is now subject to doubt."[24]

Thus, all four of SIS's main sources prior to the war proved to be reliable overall; the problem with this stable of agents was not wholesale inaccuracy, but rather hearsay reporting by one and reporting on behalf of an unreliable subagent on the part of another. Viewed in terms of the quality assurance function of the Requirements mechanism of SIS, it should have been apparent that both the first and second dominant sources were reporting in part at second hand. But were the reports properly tagged?

There has been a reasonably clear picture of UK HUMINT reporting procedure in the public domain for more than a decade. In 1993, an intelligence furor flared up in the media, driven by the prosecution of senior managers in Matrix-Churchill, one of a number of firms engaged in the export of dual-use technologies to Ba'athist Iraq. During the trial, it transpired that the managing director, Paul Henderson, had been an information source for SIS (and earlier for MI5), reporting on Iraqi weapons development programs. As a consequence, SIS and MI5 agent-handling techniques came under public scrutiny as operational reports were identified by the defense and submitted as evidence. The material submitted included the contact notes made by individual case officers after meeting with agents and the subsequent source reports based on the contact notes or other agent communications. Reporting procedures were made clear, including the requirement to distinguish between firsthand factual reporting, secondhand and hearsay information, and information that expressed an opinion or interpretation on the part of the source.[25]

Iraq reporting appears to have followed these practices. According to Butler, reports from the second dominant source's subsource did indeed go out with a rider alerting recipients to a question mark about the objectivity and reliability of that subagent's information.

Sixth source: Evaluating the sixth and final source is a somewhat complicated matter. At various points, the Butler report refers to an individual "source" and to an alleged "subsource" who appears to have been part of a larger subagent network. Butler's description of the sixth source runs as follows:

[24] Butler, 100.

[25] See, for example, David Leigh, *Betrayed: The Real Story of the Matrix-Churchill Trial* (London: Bloomsbury, 1993), 133, 135. The contact notes/source report procedures elaborated during the Matrix-Churchill trial and subsequent inquiry were specifically those of the Security Service, but standards and procedures in the two agencies are necessarily similar in this regard. Matrix-Churchill was one of a series of such prosecutions that eventually prompted a judicial inquiry by Sir Richard Scott. The Scott investigation was the most transparent inquiry into intelligence activities in the UK until the Hutton inquiry a decade later. See Richard Scott, *Report of the Inquiry into the Export of Defence Equipment and Dual-Use Goods to Iraq and Related Prosecutions* (London: HMSO, 1996), 5 vols., plus index and CD ROM.

Finally in mid-September 2002 SIS issued a report, described as being from a "new source on trial," on Iraqi production of chemical and biological agents. Although this report was received too late for inclusion in the JIC assessment [on Iraq] of 9 September, it did provide significant assurance to those drafting the government's dossier that active, current production of chemical and biological weapons was taking place. A second report from the new source, about the production of a particular chemical agent, was received later in September 2002. In July 2003, however, SIS withdrew the two reports because the sourcing chain had by then been discredited. SIS also interviewed the alleged subsource for the intelligence after the war, who denied having ever provided the information in the reports. We note, therefore, that the two reports from this source, including one which was important in the closing stages of production of the Government's September Dossier, must now be treated as unsafe.[26]

In sum, the stable of SIS sources in Iraq was hardly as strong as the JIC assessments and, more critically, the September Dossier suggested, but neither was it as catastrophically poor as has been suggested in the media. The fluctuation in the first dominant source's reports between direct knowledge and hearsay is typical of human sources. For example, a Soviet source working for the CIA and SIS known for his

---

[26] Butler, 100–101, emphasis in the original.

> ## SIS sources were not as strong as the JIC assessments suggested, but neither were they catastrophically poor.

thousands of photographed documents also provided political assessments and interpretations that were so idiosyncratic and colored by his hostility to the Soviet regime that both agencies disseminated the two kinds of products under different cryptonyms.[27] Likewise, as far back as the 1930s, SIS agent runners like Leslie Nicholson, who did not even have the benefit of something like the contemporary Intelligence Officers New Entry Course, were acutely aware of the difficulties and uncertainties of dealing with networks of subagents.[28] So there were good reasons behind SIS's placing dominant source one's hearsay information and source two's subagent reporting in parentheses; this did not necessarily impugn the source's direct reporting. And, of course, both other main sources have retained their credibility with SIS and the Butler review team.

---

[27] Jerrold Shecter and Peter Deriabin, *The Spy Who Saved the World: How a Soviet Colonel Changed the Course of the Cold War* (London: Brassey's, 1995), 333–35.

[28] See Nicholson, writing as John Whitwell, *British Agent* (London: William Kimber, 1967). In particular, Nicholson provides an instructive account of his ALEX network, identified by appended numbers such as ALEX-1, ALEX-2, and so forth, 85–86.

As a result, SIS had two unqualified good sources (*four* and *five*), two bad sources (*three* and *six*), and two sources that were a bit of both, but good at least when sticking to first-hand knowledge (*one* and *two*). *However, how these sources were factored into the national assessment process at the JIC level and represented to the public in the September Dossier is an entirely different matter.*

Britain's Analysis on Iraq

Lord Butler is quite specific about how the various sources in SIS's Iraqi stable were factored into JIC deliberations. On Iraqi ballistic missile programs, a JIC *assessment of 10 February 2001* asserted "We know that Iraq has retained key components of disassembled 640-km-range Al Hussein missiles. Recent intelligence suggests that they may have assembled some of these." According to Butler, this estimate rested partly on prior (worst case) estimates that Iraq had concealed missile components, but also on:

> *. . . three pieces of human intelligence from three separate sources on Iraqi possession of Al Hussein missiles. One of those sources provided the actual number of "up to 20 missiles" being concealed, which was subsequently reflected in all future JIC estimates . . . . that source was, in our view in a position to comment authoritatively; and we have established that he reported reliably both before and after*

> ## 66
> ## The intelligence applied to mainly historical activity of the Iraqi regime.
> ## 99

the report. But we note that he was passing on the comments of a subsource, who reported only once. SIS had not, by the time we finished our Review, been able to contact the subsource to validate the reliability of his reporting.[29]

In a *10 May 2001 assessment* of Iraqi nuclear, biological, chemical, and ballistic missile programs, the JIC cautioned in the body of the report that it had "no clear intelligence" on Iraqi capabilities; however, in its Key Judgement on the nuclear matter, it stated that there was evidence of an Iraqi program to acquire dual-use items potentially applicable to a nuclear weapons program and to conducting unspecified nuclear-related research that could contribute to a break-out production capability *if sanctions were lifted.* Commenting on this, Butler observes:

[The] judgement was based on two human intelligence reports, both from new sources and neither speaking from direct, current experience. Unusually in the nuclear field, we conclude that those reports were given more weight in the JIC assessment than they could reasonably bear.[30]

In the same report, the assessment of Iraqi chemical weapons (CW) capability was that "we believe Iraq retains some production equipment, stocks of CW precursors, agents and weapons." But the assessment simultaneously warned that "intelligence of other CW activity, including possible weaponisation, is less clear." According to Lord Butler, the HUMINT sources behind this estimate consisted of "a single report from a new source who reported details of a project *three years earlier* to integrate the nerve agent VX into rocket artillery warheads and the subsequent filling of 60 warheads" and "a further single report from a new source, passing on the comments of a subsource that he had been part of a project to produce the nerve agent VX in the period to 1998, *again three years earlier.*" As Butler observes rather sharply, "the intelligence applied to mainly historical (as opposed to current) activity and, even so, was by no means conclusive."[31]

The JIC produced another *assessment on 21 August 2002*, titled "Saddam's Diplomatic and Military Options." The report, prepared in response to a requirement from the Ministry of Defence, warned that "although

we have little intelligence on Iraq's CBW doctrine, and know little about Iraq's CBW work since late 1998, we judge it likely that Saddam would order the use of CBW against coalition forces at some point."[32] Lord Butler points out that, given the context of the requirement, "the Key Judgements of that assessment would rightly have been prepared on a precautionary basis . . . when set against intelligence on Iraqi programmes contained in advice for Ministers in March, the [August] JIC assessment reflected more firmly the premise that Iraq had chemical and biological weapons and would use them in war."[33] Significantly, the conclusions "were based in part on one human intelligence report from one source *but mainly the JIC's own judgements.*"[34] In other words, the 21 August assessment was not a predictive one, but a speculative one that necessarily had to employ a worst-case approach and err on the side of caution.

The 9 September Assessment

The *next assessment, dated 9 September 2002*, addressed "Iraqi Use of Chemical and Biological Weapons—Possible Scenarios." This estimate, which served as the main source for the unclassified September Dossier, reflects caveats similar to those of the other estimates, but, significantly, reached much firmer con-

---

[29] Butler, 61.

[30] Ibid., 56. It is hard to reconcile the "two new sources" given here with the stocktaking of SIS assets presented earlier. One might indeed be the subagent to the second dominant source, but the other last minute agent mentioned on a previous page did not report until September; therefore, the second new source given here must not have been in the Iraq stable. He may have been either an émigré or part of the reporting chain to the September new source.

[31] Ibid., 58.

[32] Ibid., 73.

[33] Ibid., 72.

[34] Ibid., 73, emphasis added.

clusions than prior reports. It warned that "Intelligence remains limited and Saddam's own unpredictability complicates judgements about Iraqi use of these weapons" and that "Much of the paper is necessarily based on judgement and assessment" rather than hard evidence. Despite this, it also asserted, in apparent self-contradiction, that "Recent intelligence casts light on Iraq's holdings of weapons of mass destruction and its doctrine for using them" and, with unprecedented confidence, that "Iraq has chemical and biological weapons capability and Saddam is prepared to use it." The assessment further claimed that "other recent intelligence indicates that production of chemical and biological weapons is taking place." Again somewhat inconsistently, the supporting discussion held that Iraq could produce chemical agents "within weeks" and biological agents "within days," and that Baghdad had retained "up to 20 al Husseins."[35] These points were consistent with the more tentative earlier reports, which had placed emphasis not on stockpiles in hand, but on research and development and a latent, but possibly growing, "break-out capability" to kickstart chemical and biological agent production and weaponization programs once sanctions were lifted.

The Butler *Review* details the sources underpinning the 9 September assessment, and hence

---

[35] Ibid., 73–74.

> ## " The more definite judgments inside the assessment were based on new intelligence. "

the published Dossier, in considerable detail, and it is worth quoting the review at some length on this.

The more definite judgements inside the assessment were based on the receipt of significant new intelligence in August and September 2002, in response to the routine requirement on SIS to obtain information to support the drafting of JIC assessments . . . . Four reports were received in total, from three sources, which were influential in the JIC's assessment.

The first provided material from a range of original informants via an intermediary source. We have noted, however, that the individual informants did not confirm directly that Iraq had chemical weapons. They came from senior Iraqi officials who were believed at the time to have direct knowledge of Iraq's intentions, use, deployment and concealment of chemical weapons, but were based for most of the informants on an assumption (not direct knowledge) that Iraq had such weapons.

The second and third were from a source who had previously reported reliably and who continued to do so in the following months. This source, too, could not confirm from direct knowledge that Iraq had chemical weapons, resting upon

"common knowledge" within his circle *that chemical agent production was taking place. The second report from this source seems to us to duplicate much of the first.*

The fourth was a single report, from a reliable and established source reporting a new subsource who did not subsequently provide any further reporting, which was described as "confirming" the intelligence on Iraqi mobile biological agent production facilities received from [CIA]. Contrary to the JIC view at the time, we believe that this report would have been more accurately described as "complementary" to, rather than "confirming," it.[36]

Unsurprisingly, the Butler team concluded: "We were struck by the relative thinness of the intelligence base supporting the greater firmness of the JIC's judgements on Iraqi production and possession of biological weapons, especially the inferential nature of much of it."

The *Review* identified one last source during the final interval before the war. This informant, who played a central role during much of the postwar debate about the quality of the raw intelligence fed into the estimates of Iraqi WMD, was the

---

[36] Ibid., 74–75, emphasis added. Regarding the first reporting chain, the *Review* includes a footnote that refers to the summary of SIS sources, which notes that "We were told by SIS during the course of our Review that there is now doubt about the reliability of this reporting chain and hence of the reports derived from it."

> ## " The '45-minute claim' acquired a central role in the controversy over the 'sexing up' of intelligence. "

source of a report received after 9 September, during the drafting of the September Dossier. The report proved especially controversial because it was used to quash objections to the wording of the Dossier raised by Dr. Brian Jones and the analysts at the Directorate of Scientific and Technical Intelligence at the Defence Intelligence Service (DIS).

Just before the 9 September assessment was completed, an SIS source, viewed at the time as having a "proven and reliable" track record,[37] provided information that unspecified Iraqi chemical weapons could be prepared for use in "45 minutes or less." The source in question may indeed have been individually reliable, but he was a subagent in a rather long reporting chain. His "45-minute claim" played a relatively minor role in the 9 September JIC assessment. However, due partly to its inherently alarming nature, partly to vague wording that amplified its alarming nature, and partly to ill-considered repetition in the September Dossier, the 45-minute claim acquired a central role in the subsequent controversy over the "sexing up" of intelligence by the government, the accusations of BBC journalist Andrew Gilligan, and the suicide of Dr. David Kelly. During the postwar validation review, reports Butler, "SIS interviewed the alleged subsource . . . who

denied ever having provided the information in the reports." The claim evidently had been fabricated by an intervening member of the reporting chain, based on a Soviet-era military handbook specification.[38]

Before the Iraq invasion, analysts at DIS had been dubious about the validity of some of the HUMINT reporting—including the 45-minute claim—and the strength of the conclusions that could be reached on the basis of that reporting. On seeing a draft of the September Dossier, Jones prepared a memorandum to his line manager that challenged the conclusion that Iraq had chemical agents in hand. He argued that "We have not seen intelligence which we believe 'shows' that Iraq has continued to produce CW agent in 1998–2002, although *in our judgement* it has probably done so." Jones's objections were overruled by the deputy chief of defence intelligence, in part because of the time pressure under which the Dossier was being drafted. Another factor working against Jones, however, was a report from the last-minute source that supposedly corroborated the 45-minute claim.[39]

This brand new source "reported that production of biological and chemical agents had been accelerated by the Iraqi regime."[40] Jones had been denied access to this report on the grounds that the author was a "new source on trial." In giving evidence to the Butler team, SIS Chief Sir Richard Dearlove explained that it was SIS practice to limit the circle of individuals indoctrinated into any new source during the agent's "initial, very sensitive period of development."[41] As a consequence, dissemination and evaluation of the new agent's report was confined to SIS's own technical experts who "took a preliminary and provisional view that the report should be issued, as being from 'a new source on trial.'"

The restricted dissemination in and of itself indicates that this last minute information was hardly from the sort of tried and proven line of reporting that would ordinarily carry enough weight to tip the analytical scales in one direction or another. There

---

[37] Richard Dearlove, "Evidence to Parliamentary Foreign Affairs Committee," FAC/3/26 (2003).

[38] Butler, 111, 127.

[39] Quoted in Butler, 138. Jones's concerns were first publicly addressed in an elliptical style in the Parliamentary Intelligence and Security Committee's report *Iraqi Weapons of Mass Destruction: Intelligence and Assessments* (London: TSO, 2003), 29–30. They then became a significant feature in the evidence compiled during the Hutton inquiry when Jones himself was invited to testify—see oral evidence to Lord Hutton's Inquiry, at: http://www.the-huttoninquiry.org.uk/content/transcripts/hearingtrans28.htm—and then in still more direct detail in his article "Hutton Report: The Aftermath," *The Independent,* 4 February 2004.

[40] Butler, 75.

[41] Ibid., 138.

> ## "
> ## Information from the new source was mishandled at two points.
> ## "

appears, therefore, to have been a mishandling of the new source's information at two points: The first, as Lord Butler points out, was the unwillingness to make untested and uncertain materials available to "the few people in the UK intelligence community able to form all-round, professional technical judgements on its reliability and significance"; the second was the fact that, despite qualifications placed upon the source by SIS's own technical validation personnel, this source was viewed by senior SIS and DIS managers at the JIC as being sufficient to negate Jones's concerns. Rather than dogmatically following a source protection protocol, argues Butler, senior managers in the DIS and SIS should have "made arrangements for the intelligence to be shown to DIS experts instead of making their own judgements on its significance."[42] Significant fault therefore rested with senior SIS and DIS officials—evidently at the JIC level—in their representation of, and the relative weight given to, this source, as well as other aspects of HUMINT reporting on Iraqi nonconventional weapons.

Stepping Back

What pressures, assumptions, or incentives may have propelled the top intelligence management and analytical team in the UK government to place such excessive weight on sources? Lord But-

ler reached a series of key conclusions about the validation and assessment of intelligence at both the agency and JIC levels. While judging that the use of émigré sources was not a significant problem, the Butler review raised concerns about the reliance on subagent networks with long reporting chains: "Even when there were sources who were shown to be reliable in some areas of reporting, they had in other areas of intelligence concern where they did not have direct knowledge to draw on subsources or sub-subsources."

The inclusion of insufficiently validated subsource reporting was no doubt driven by the fact that "agents who were known to be reliable were asked to report on issues going well beyond their normal territory." Also, "because of the scarcity of sources and the urgent requirement for intelligence, more credence was given to untried agents than would normally be the case."[43]

These problems put strains on the SIS collection and reporting system that should have been detectable by Requirements Sections performing their quality-control function effectively. But, as Butler makes evident,

Requirements was so diminished, it could not do so.[44]

Throughout its assessments after the first Gulf war, the JIC had sustained *suspicions* that there might be weapons, components, and precursors that were slipping beneath the horizon of UN inspections and the available hard intelligence.[45] These preconceptions that the weapons were there led the JIC to an overly robust interpretation of current reporting. Instead of being derived primarily from the evidence at hand, JIC *judgments* in 2002 were formed with strong reference to Saddam Hussein's prior history of WMD production, concealment, and use. Assessments, Lord Butler concludes, tended to be "coloured by over-reaction to previous errors," and there was a definite process of what the US Senate report termed "layering"—whereby "over-cautious or worst-case estimates shorn of their caveats" were carried over from one assessment to another, becoming "prevailing wisdom." In other words, the preconceptions contributed to a level of groupthink where the JIC was looking less for indications of what might be the case than for what they expected to be the case.

It is significant to note, however, that, even with the layering and groupthink, the JIC was scrupulous about caveating its esti-

---

42 Ibid., 138–39.

43 Ibid., 108.

44 Ibid., 109.
45 The persistence of these suspicions is a recurrent theme throughout the Butler *Review*.

mates and acknowledging lacunae in its data set, confining itself to asserting nothing more than suspicion, at least until the 9 September assessment. But even the September assessment was qualified in terms of the available intelligence and the JIC's reliance on judgment—inference and informed speculation—as the basis for its firmest and least defensible conclusion about Iraqi possession of WMD.

Fixing the Machine

It might be invidious to observe that SIS's six sources in Iraq, for all their variable quality, were six more than certain key allied intelligence services had, but it is important to keep in mind that SIS *was* successfully recruiting sources in a very hard target state. Nonetheless, although reporting was strong in some areas, there can be no doubt that very serious problems existed with respect to the quality of raw human intelligence reporting on Iraqi nonconventional weapons programs.

One must be cautious about reaching overly strong or sweeping judgments on the basis of the limited information. While SIS certainly had more penetration operations running against China and Russia in the Cold War than against Iraq in absolute numbers, it would be instructive to see how the ratio between strong, variable, and weak sources compared with that in Iraq. Moreover, the Butler *Review* does not give a compara-

> ## " The JIC made stronger judgments on Iraq than available sourcing could support. "

ble stocktaking of the number/quality distribution of the sources in hand for those relative successes against Iran, Libya, North Korea, and the Pakistani arms network. Did having six sources—with reporting that was 33 percent solid, 33 percent variable, and 33 percent weak—constitute a reasonable, poor, or indifferent performance against a regional counter-proliferation requirement? This evaluation cannot be confidently made based on the volume and quality of information available through the Butler review and other inquiries that followed the Iraq invasion.

What is evident, however, is that the JIC made stronger judgments on Iraq than available sourcing could support. Therefore, the question that has to be asked is what went wrong on SIS's Requirements side that led to the failure to adequately assert and sustain the distinction between sheep- and goat-quality reporting and monitor the use of that reporting in the national analytical process in the Cabinet Office.

What went wrong was not a lack of sources but a failure to adequately lift the intelligence signal out of the background noise and make sure that the signal reached consumers, analysts, and

decisionmakers with the required clarity. *The real failure of the SIS validation system was not the failure to provide reliable reporting on Iraq, but, rather, a failure to effectively separate the reliable reporting from the less so.*

This failure has to be seen not as a short-term breakdown in the SIS validation machinery resulting from cutbacks in the 1990s, as Butler contends, but as the culmination of a steady weakening of the Requirements mechanism for handling tasking, dissemination, and validation, since 1974. The abolition of a separate identity for Requirements was accompanied by successive moves to push responsibility "further down the organisational pyramid," as one officer put it.[46] The question has to be asked how far down can one push a function in an organizational hierarchy before it is deprived of any influential voice at the decisionmaking levels. As the Butler team observed:

> *The quality assurance function of the SIS "Requirements" officer . . . became subjected to the operational imperative of the team leader [Controller] to produce results. At the same time, we were told [by one SIS official], "Requirements" posts were increasingly staffed by more junior officers as experienced staff were put into improving the operational teeth of the Service. Their ability to*

---

[46] Confidential briefing by former senior SIS officer, 19 July 2005.

challenge the validity of cases and their reporting was correspondingly reduced. [47]

These sentiments were echoed by a second interviewee, who expressed concern that the "staff effort overall, and the number of experienced case officers in particular" applied to the Middle East and Global and Functional Controllerates was "too thin to support SIS' responsibilities" so that "source validation, especially on Iraq, had suffered as a consequence of both problems with what were in the witness's view sources with dubious motivation *being overgraded for reliability*."[48]

An oft-heard refrain in US intelligence literature is that what is needed most is not more collection but, rather, more analysis. Much the same point seems to apply to validation in the British system: Validation is not highly manpower-intensive, but it makes a disproportionately important difference to the quality of finished intelligence. Because this is a counterintuitive conclusion, it is easy to sympathize with Dearlove's observation during the Butler review:

It is very, very difficult, particularly when the pressure on the Service is to produce good intelligence, to put your officers who are the only ones who can do production as well into the Requirements tasks. I accept problems and the fact that in an

---

> ## SIS may not be truly effective until Requirements regains an independent presence on the Board of Directors.

ideal world you would only staff your Requirements desks with very experienced operational officers. In practice that is not possible.[49]

The problem, of course, is that this trade-off of validation against operational capability had been made not once but at least three times between 1974 and 1994, leaving very little slack in the system when it came under increased pressure from consumers between the autumns of 2001 and 2002.

One of Lord Butler's few explicit recommendations on reform was to "urge the Chief of SIS to ensure that this task [validation] is properly resourced and organised . . . and we think that it would be appropriate if the [Parliamentary] Intelligence and Security Committee were to monitor this."[50] In mid-January 2005, there was a flurry of UK press interest in a briefing from the prime minister's spokesman to the effect that SIS had reinstituted the position of Deputy Director Requirements as part of the implementation of the Butler Review's recommendations.[51] What this reform does, however,

is simply return Requirements to its previous, diminished status quo ante of 1993, under the equivalent of a Deputy Director subordinate to D/PR.[52] Responsibility for representing SIS on the JIC's Current Intelligence Groups also remains to be returned to the Requirements Sections. This is necessary not only to ensure the most objective possible representation of SIS product in the assessment drafting process, but also to restore to Requirements the authority of speaking on behalf of the Assessments Staff within SIS.

However much SIS's own senior officials may believe that Requirements has remained undiminished,[53] it is evident that it did not have the voice and the authority at the top level in SIS to prevent the agency's product from being oversold in the JIC's deliberations on Iraq. As a consequence, SIS may not remain truly effectively reformed until quality control and the Requirements side once again have their own independent presence on that agency's Board of Directors.

---

[47] Butler, 103.

[48] Ibid., emphasis added.

[49] Quoted in Butler, 104.

[50] Ibid., 109.

[51] For an example of the caliber of press response, see Richard Norton-Taylor, "MI6 acts to curb rows over spying," *The Guardian,* 12 January 2005. For a detailed and well-informed account, see Gordon Corera, "UK Makes Changes to Secret Intelligence Service," *Jane's Intelligence Review,* February 2005: 48–51.

[52] Confidential conversation with senior SIS official, 19 January 2005.

[53] See, for example, Sir Richard Dearlove's remarks to the review panel on this question, in Butler, 102.

Can the USG and NGOs Do More?

Ellen B. Laipson

> " The information-sharing dynamics between state and nonstate actors can be a useful window into the post-Cold War world. "

Ellen B. Laipson heads the Henry L. Stimson Center, a think tank that focuses on international security issues. She served in the US government for 25 years, including as vice chairman of the National Intelligence Council.

Over the past decade and a half, three phenomena have expanded dramatically: the availability of information through the diffusion of information technology; the role of nongovernmental organizations (NGOs) as important players in international affairs; and the demand for international engagement in failed or weak states, some having suffered from devastating conflicts. These three facts interact and raise a number of issues for US policymakers and for the Intelligence Community. This article examines how information-sharing between the government and the NGO sector has evolved and considers whether changes in that relationship are warranted, even needed, for accomplishing the shared objective of improved international response to conflicts and other crises in weak states.[1]

[1] Research for this article was supported by the Center for the Study of Intelligence and the Office of Transnational Issues, CIA. The Henry L. Stimson Center in Washington, DC, sponsored two workshops in 2005 to examine these issues: The author met with NGO leaders on 16 February; and NGO representatives and US government officials convened on 28 April. Only the author is responsible for the views expressed. The author wishes to thank Anna Tunkel, a Stimson Center intern, for her able assistance.

Uncharted Territory

Improvement of information-sharing has become the clarion call of many recent criticisms of US government performance. The 9/11 Commission called for improved information-sharing within the government, concluding that the failure to prevent the terrorist attacks on the United States was due, in part, to the hoarding of information by different components of the complex US system.[2] Similarly, the scathing reports about US intelligence performance regarding Iraq's weapons of mass destruction highlight a bureaucratic system that creates barriers to information-sharing within the executive branch, and with Congress, the public, and key partners, including coalition allies. The recently appointed Director of National Intelligence faces the challenge of creating a new culture that promotes integration of information, rather than further compartmentalization.

Information-sharing between the government and nonstate actors is a small part of this larger set of issues, but examination of

[2] *The 9/11 Commission Report: Final report of the National Commission on Terrorist Attacks upon the United States* (New York: W. W. Norton & Co., 2004), 353, 394, 401–3, 407–10.

All statements of fact, opinion, or analysis expressed in this article are those of the author. Nothing in the article should be construed as asserting or implying US government endorsement of an article's factual statements and interpretations.

> ## 66
> ## NGOs account for over 5 percent of GDP and 4 percent of employment around the world.
> ## 99

those dynamics can be a useful window into the post-Cold War, globalized world. The range of roles that nonstate actors play is wide: Some relief organizations come to humanitarian operations at their own initiative, whereas others provide logistics, transportation, medical services, and security at the request of governments or international organizations. It is often difficult to distinguish between those activities in crisis areas that are inherently governmental in nature and those that can be as easily, or perhaps even better, carried out by nongovernmental actors. The boundaries are increasingly blurred. Critical questions surface: Are governments and NGOs complementary players in crisis situations? Are they actively interdependent? Are they competitive? Do local populations distinguish between different types of relief assistance? Should they distinguish? How do NGOs balance the short-term need to get a job done (save lives, feed people), which may require working with a government, with a long-term institutional interest in retaining an independent identity?

Moreover, how does one define the information suitable for sharing? Should sensitive intelligence relating to troop deployments and the capabilities of potential combatants or spoilers of international peace operations be given out? What about knowledge of terrain, infrastructure, health and food conditions, and culture? As with intelligence-policy relationships, different play-

ers will have distinctly different definitions of what information needs to be shared or is suitable for sharing. There is strategic analysis, valuable for planning purposes at the headquarters of large organizations that deploy worldwide. There is highly perishable political information about conditions on the ground after a conflict that is critical to determining what areas are safe for humanitarian efforts. And there is fine-grained information needed for immediate triage once relief groups arrive on the ground in acute situations, where limited resources must be carefully allocated for maximum impact on saving lives.

Effective communication faces many hurdles. NGOs and affected citizens in crisis zones often assume that foreign governments have access to all possible information, when, in fact, they may not have a presence in the affected area. NGO field operatives are often already present in remote regions, but may place little priority on feeding local information to capitals and foreign governments.

Recent History

Information-sharing between the US government and NGOs has gone through various phases. For many who lived through years of

the government keeping NGOs at arms length, the "Great Lakes crisis" in Central Africa in the mid-1990s was a turning point. Washington wanted to be engaged but had few assets on the ground. The NGOs were eager to help the refugees and people displaced by the multiple, interrelated crises in Rwanda, Burundi, and the Democratic Republic of the Congo, but they needed assistance in identifying the most acute areas. Because the issues had little national security sensitivity for the United States, the government was willing to share satellite imagery (although it proved of dubious value in heavily forested areas) and other intelligence-derived information. In turn, NGOs on the ground with satellite phones and other modern means of communication were often able to send back "ground truth" reporting.

Building on the Great Lakes experience, collaboration between NGOs and military and civilian components of the government developed further in the Balkans. Human rights NGOs and US intelligence analysts found themselves working together in support of the Balkans war crimes tribunals in The Hague and other aspects of peace-building in Bosnia and Kosovo.

Subsequently, however, Iraq and, to a lesser extent, Afghanistan were setbacks in the mutual willingness to collaborate. The NGO community debated with some passion the moral and ethical dilemmas of following US troops

> ## NGOs have diverse views about cooperating with governments in post-conflict work.

into war zones when the conflicts were considered "wars of choice." Some were willing to go to Iraq if there was a humanitarian need; others found the situation highly problematic and preferred to focus on needy countries elsewhere, where the politics were easier to handle. The Bush administration's director of the Agency for International Development (AID) brought tensions to a head in the spring of 2003 when he demanded that NGOs identify their activities in Afghanistan as funded by the US government. NGO objections led conservative institutions to launch a Web site designed to monitor NGOs for their alleged liberal bias and unwillingness to adhere to current policy preferences.[3]

Tsunami relief in late 2004 was, in contrast, largely a positive story. The US military responded to NGO requests for transportation and did not seek to be in charge of operations on the ground. NGOs were pleasantly surprised that Washington was able to provide such valuable

support while permitting the NGOs to take the lead where they had the expertise to do so. But the dynamics in the tsunami case were eased by the fact that it was a purely humanitarian crisis, not fraught with the political dimensions that many post-conflict situations entail. Nonetheless, it restored some good will and collegiality and is likely to have salutary benefits for information-sharing and other forms of cooperation in future crises.

NGO Diversity

A vast literature now exists to track and assess the ever-expanding phenomenon of global civil society, including the dizzying array of organizations that can be called "nonprofit, voluntary, independent, charitable, people's, philanthropic, associational, or third sector."[4] NGOs are now an important economic player around the world, accounting for over 5 percent of the gross domestic product and over 4 percent of employment, according to the most definitive study that tracks civil society in

three dozen countries.[5] Some NGOs also take on explicitly political functions, challenging governments and international organizations when they fail to respond to a crisis and rallying citizens internationally in support of specific policies or initiatives. The 1997 grass-roots campaign to ban landmines is seen as a watershed for NGO activism and impact. Its success has strengthened the resolve of "third sector" leaders to be recognized and represented in diverse institutional settings. Some consider the rise of NGOs as an "associational revolution," comparable to the rise of the nation-state in the late 19th century.[6]

The subset of NGOs relevant to this discussion of information-sharing comprises those whose primary mission is relief, humanitarian aid, and development assistance and reconstruction. It is these NGOs who are most likely to be on the ground in times of human tragedy and post-conflict situations where information-sharing is an acute need and where the US government has often responded with a willingness to share. There are several hundred such NGOs headquartered in the United States. One umbrella organization alone—Interaction—has 160

---

[3] The AID director's comment and its aftermath are discussed in Abby Stoddard, "With Us or Against Us? NGO Neutrality on the Line," *Humanitarian Practice Network*, December 2003, found at: http://www.globalpolicy.org/ngos/fund/2003/1200against.htm. The debate over relations with occupying militaries is discussed in an essay by Hugo Slim, "With or Against? Humanitarian Agencies and Coalition CounterInsurgency," Centre for Humanitarian Dialogue, July 2004, 2–15, available at: http://www.hdcentre.org/datastore/shaping%20opinion/With%20Against%20.pdf.

[4] Some of this literature is referenced in Adil Najam, "The Four-C's of Third Sector-Government Relations: Cooperation, Confrontation, Complementarity and Co-optation," *Nonprofit Management and Leadership* 10, no. 4 (Summer 2000): 375.

[5] Lester Salamon, S. Wojciech Sokolowski, and Associates, *Global Civil Society: Dimensions of the Nonprofit Sector*, Vol. II (Bloomfield, CT: Kumarian Press, Inc., 2004), 15–17.

[6] J. N. Rosenau, "Governance in the Twenty-first Century," *Global Governance* (1995), as cited in Najam.

> ## " In the field, politics tend to give way to a focus on the immediate need. "

member groups, which vary in size and mission, but adhere to a common set of private voluntary standards. Interaction advocates on behalf of the NGO sector when there is consensus about relief and humanitarian needs.[7]

NGOs have diverse views regarding cooperation with governments in post-conflict work. Some—such as *Medecins sans Frontieres* and the International Red Cross—pride themselves on serving a completely apolitical set of objectives and feel no need to interact with governmental groups that may be in the same area. These groups establish relations with a host government as needed, presuming there is a host government, but not with foreign forces. Other NGOs—such as CARE, World Vision, Mercy Corps, and Save the Children—have contact with foreign governments as needed for security and practical reasons, but are careful to distinguish their work from that of government in their dealings with the local population.[8] Yet another group—which includes International Medical Corps and the new faith-based NGOs—has no reservations about cooperating with foreign governments and forces. They see themselves as implementers of policies decided and funded in the capi-

tals of wealthy nations for the shared purpose of relieving suffering in developing countries or regions in crisis.

Money is one of the factors that create the distinctions. Few NGOs are able to fund their activities entirely out of private donations. World Vision—now the largest US NGO, with annual revenues of $700 million—and Oxfam-US, for example, receive about 20 percent of their revenue from the government, mainly from AID's Office of Foreign Disaster Assistance (OFDA). At the other end of the spectrum, International Medical Corps receives about 80 percent of its funding from government sources. NGOs also distinguish between their relationship with OFDA, which they find to be a like-minded, apolitical, humanitarian agency, and their contacts with other parts of the government that advocate a political or policy agenda and want NGOs to associate themselves with it.

Security is another dividing line. Some NGOs seek an association with the US military in crisis zones, believing that a cooperative relationship will serve to protect their civilian workers. NGOs with a long history of independence tend to be more sensitive about preserving their autonomy, judging that too much association with a foreign mili-

tary power—such as coalition forces in Afghanistan—actually increases their security vulnerability. Many NGOs have a deep belief that local populations will see them as politically acceptable even when their workers are the same nationality as an occupying force. This may be true when an NGO has a long track record in a particular country, as many NGOs did in Afghanistan. One of the painful lessons of Iraq for NGO and UN workers, however, has been that a violent fringe of the local population has not made such a distinction, and foreign nationals working for NGOs have been targeted by insurgent groups.[9]

Different Cultures

NGOs' ability to obtain information needed to plan and deploy humanitarian workers to crisis zones has improved with the spread of information technology and the growing size, sophistication, and professionalism of the "third sector." As a result, NGOs place a lower priority on information-sharing than they did in the mid-1990s. Interest in sharing may also have declined because of perceived political costs of appearing too close to controversial US policies and a perception that the information flow is lop-

---

[7] See http://www.interaction.org for more information about Interaction's advocacy role and the coordination of shared standards for voluntary work.

[8] One NGO leader has estimated that 10 large agencies in this middle group do 80 percent of the emergency work.

[9] The bombing of UN headquarters in Baghdad in July 2003 led to increased attention to providing security for NGO workers. Many NGOs now hire private security firms to advise and protect workers in post-conflict situations where violence is still common.

sided in favor of the government. This is particularly true of information-sharing in capitals, where NGO-government discussions of a current or looming crisis are often fraught with uncertainties about how the United States will respond and are at the mercy of the political environment in which such decisions are being made. Once relief operations are underway in the field, the politics tend to give way to a focus on the immediate need.

Different cultural approaches to information also affect the priority given to seeking information-sharing relationships. Professionals in humanitarian organizations are action-oriented individuals, who develop highly pragmatic information strategies intended to support immediate needs. They are unlikely to allocate a lot of time to deep analytic work during the preparation phase of a deployment. Some NGO professionals are indeed country experts, or acquire unique and valuable regional insights by virtue of extended deployments in remote places, but many more are generalists with respect to geographic expertise. The US government's analytic cadres, by contrast, have information as their métier and place value on deep expertise. For them, trading in information is an end in itself, not a means to an end.

Barriers between NGOs and the US military are also formidable due to distinct organizational cultures and different time-horizons.[10] The military is

> ## "
> ## Most NGO information systems in the field are not organized for easy sharing.
> ## "

hierarchical, relies on doctrinal publications, expects discipline and conformity from its troops, and is heavily trained.[11] NGOs decentralize authority for field operations, do not develop standard manuals, value independence, and train on the spot. Nonetheless, on a number of occasions, NGOs and US military officers deployed to crisis areas have developed ad hoc collaborative arrangements for information-sharing based on mutual respect and, at the personal level, a great capacity to work together.[12]

New Directions in Information Management

Most NGOs report that information flows generally work better in the field than they do in capitals and at headquarters. Need is

---

[10] A vignette from the post-September 11 world illustrates some of the sensitivities: Secretary of State Colin Powell, in a speech delivered at the State Department on 26 October 2001, extolled the virtues of government working with nongovernmental organizations, saying: "I am serious about making sure we have the best relationship with the NGOs who are such a *force multiplier* for us—such an important part of our *combat team*" (emphasis added). For the former military officer, the use of such terminology was intended as a high compliment; but the NGOs present cringed at the linkage between their work and the political and military objectives of the government "combat team."

a great motivator to help people focus on their specific information requirements. But information "systems" in the field tend to be informal, personality-dependent, and not organized in a way that can easily be shared with parent organizations, governments, or other NGOs. Some NGOs concerned about the lack of effective information management in field operations have begun to develop ideas and implement pilot projects to explore new approaches. Examples include:

International Crisis Group. Ten years old this year, ICG was created to provide non-government analysis and advocacy to "prevent and resolve deadly crisis." It now has over 100 staff members on five continents and its field-based political analysts have become vital sources of information for both NGOs and governments considering deploying groups to crisis zones. While its mission includes advocacy of government engagement in information-sharing, its own data and

---

[11] See Melinda Hofstetter, Center for Disaster Management and Humanitarian Assistance, "Cross Cultural Relations between Civilian and Military Organizations," Tulane University, Washington, DC, Power Point presentation, date unknown. There is a growing literature on military-NGO ties, where information-sharing is covered as a subsidiary issue. See, for example, Daniel Byman, "Uncertain Partners: NGOs and the Military," *Survival* 43, no. 2 (Summer 2001): 87–114; and Capt. Chris Seiple, "Window into an Age of Windows: The US Military and the NGOs," *Marine Corps Gazette* (April 1999): 63–71.

analysis are considered by some NGOs to be of such high quality and timeliness that its reports serve as substitutes for information that earlier would have been sought from government.

Vietnam Veterans of America Foundation. The VVAF has played a pioneering role in developing information systems to support NGOs in the field. In collaboration with the UN's Office of Coordination of Humanitarian Affairs, VVAF deployed humanitarian information management officers to Iraq in early 2003 and created a unique information hub for all data relating to landmines.[13] This project, called iMMAP (Information Management and Mine Action Programs), gathered data on mines

---

[12] One recent work that focuses on information and intelligence is Ben de Jong, Wies Platje, and Robert David Steele, eds., *Peacekeeping Intelligence: Emerging Concepts for the Future* (Oakton, VA: OSS International Press, 2003). See also Michael Smith and Melinda Hofstetter, "Conduit or Cul-de-Sac? Information Flow in Civil-Military Operations," *Joint Forces Quarterly* (Spring 1999): 100–105. Over the past several years, the US Institute of Peace, in partnership with Finland's Crisis Management Initiative, has explored in-depth ways to enhance interoperability of communications systems and establish common categories of information to share. They have addressed such concrete issues as the need for an international convention to allow international organizations to transport and use telecommunications equipment in crisis situations exempt from certain regulations.

[13] VVAF has also worked on mine issues (conducting surveys, training, providing maps for humanitarian workers and host governments, etc.) in Kosovo, Yemen, Chad, Thailand, Afghanistan, and Lebanon.

> ## 66
> **It is at the 'zero point' of a crisis, where governments and NGOs most need to pool information.**
>
> ## 99

from all possible sources and shared them with the humanitarian community. iMMAP produced landmine and unexploded ordinance threat maps, humanitarian operations maps, and security assessment maps. In an agile and effective way, the NGO was able to collate information from international organizations, the foreign militaries in the theater, and humanitarian groups, and disseminate an all-source integrated product back to all parties. iMMAP programs currently run in 14 countries, including the United States, where military officers are trained in mine awareness and learn to coordinate their work with international and nongovernmental groups. Building local capacity, the VVAF often leaves information technology hardware behind and trains local personnel to keep systems operating after a crisis abates and NGO needs shift.

Inter-NGO Collaboration. In capitals and in the field, NGOs are developing increasingly robust mechanisms to share information quickly for new deployments. For example, officers in Washington and other capitals adjust work hours to be on the same schedule as field operations to facilitate communication. Through Interaction, the

NGO clearing house, coordination meetings permit a regular sharing and pooling of information from the field, although many field operatives still assign back-briefing the home office a relatively low-priority. Some NGOs have experimented with deploying an information officer as part of a field team, but most are constrained by funding. NGOs have begun to add the information function to budgets submitted to OFDA and other government funders. Such an approach would also provide a natural link to government information providers and facilitate communication between field operations and decisionmakers in capitals or at UN headquarters.

Web-based Information Providers. These are often run by NGOs with funding from the UN, AID, and other donors.

• *Integrated Regional Information Networks (IRIN)*, for example, was established in 1994 as a result of the Great Lakes crisis. IRIN has pioneered the use of e-mail to deliver and receive information from remote regions where humanitarian operations are underway, with the goal of providing universal access to timely, strategic information to support conflict resolution by countering misinformation and propaganda. It currently has offices in the Ivory Coast, South Africa, Pakistan, and the United States (New York), and its e-mail service reaches 100,000 subscribers daily.

- *Relief Web* was created in October 1996 as an electronic gateway to documents and maps on humanitarian emergencies and disasters. Administered by the UN's Office for the Coordination of Humanitarian Affairs (OCHA) and funded, at least initially, by AID, it is nonetheless considered independent. It pools information from government, academic, and NGO sources, yielding a database with over 300,000 maps and documents dating back to 1981. Relief Web reaches 70,000 e-mail subscribers, in addition to those who access the information through the Web.

- *Humanitarian Information Centres* embodies a concept put into practice in 1999 in Kosovo, which has been adapted to help in Eritrea, Afghanistan, Palestine, Iraq, and Liberia. HIC focuses on maps and other concrete, actionable data, such as the availability of health facilities, curfew tracking, and drought information. It also provides training in Geographic Information Systems and "internet café" services for humanitarian workers to access HIC information. It contributes to capacity building for the local society, since departing international humanitarian workers often train local counterparts and leave their computers behind.

> ❝
>
> **Sharing with nonstate groups is not natural behavior for intelligence professionals.**
>
> ❞

Challenges Remain

These NGO endeavors are important and useful, but gaps in information support remain. For the most part, the Web-based systems do not provide critical analysis of the politics of a crisis or insight into security conditions that would permit an NGO to determine whether the situation on the ground is safe for its workers. When a crisis develops in an area where neither diplomats nor NGOs have an established presence, filling these information gaps can be a critical factor in whether humanitarian assistance will reach the populations most in need.

It is at this initial stage, the "zero point" of a crisis, where governments and NGOs most need to pool information. Often NGOs have been engaged nearby in a failing state or crisis-prone region and have accumulated knowledge before foreign governments become focused on the area. If relationships and communication ties exist, NGOs can play a vital role in getting government officials up to speed quickly, especially important during policy deliberations. It can also work the other way. Through briefings, analysts in Washington or US embassies can help NGOs learn quickly about the physical and political terrain.

The crisis in Darfur, Sudan, provides an illustrative example of the boundaries of NGO-government information-sharing. NGO leaders turned to governments for help in identifying the locations of burned villages and were quite satisfied with the information they received (derived from satellite imagery).[14] But data on aid to the rebels and arms deliveries were not forthcoming, presumably because they were either unavailable or considered politically sensitive. Over time, the NGOs deployed to Darfur will almost certainly have a clearer sense of conditions on the ground than the US government, whose officials have visited the conflict zone but are not posted there. The lasting value of such ground truth to aid donors and governments will depend on establishing good communications links and relationships.

Afghanistan illustrates other restraints. US analysts focused on force protection have been wary of sharing with NGOs out of concern that information indicating military plans or presence might endanger the forces—not because NGOs would intentionally share the information for that purpose, but because the information could be misused by local civilians involved in the humanitarian work.

---

[14] Smart information-sharing permitted the information, not the imagery itself, to be passed to the NGOs, which would not have in-house capacity to exploit imagery.

Information-sharing and Intelligence

Sharing information with nongovernmental groups and international organizations is not natural behavior for US intelligence professionals. Over the past decade or more, however, some new habits have been forming. Sharing usually is initiated by a request from policymakers, an important sign that providing the information is consistent with the administration's foreign affairs objectives. On occasion, the sharing of information about an emerging crisis *becomes* the policy. In the absence of a political consensus or when action by the United States is unlikely, information-sharing constitutes one way in which Washington can be seen as helpful and supportive of the efforts of others internationally. Sometimes, however, that willingness to share is not matched by actually having quality information or analysis available to be shared, which can raise false expectations and damage nascent relationships.

NGOs often are not the intended beneficiaries of official sharing policies. The United Nations, from its peacekeepers and humanitarian organizations to war crimes tribunals, is the more likely customer. But once material is prepared for the UN community, there is often a demand to share it with the UN's partners in the NGO world.

In some cases, the Intelligence Community has shared strategic analyses directly with nongovern-

> ## "
> ## Some NGOs have complained that what the US shares has already been in the news.
> ## "

mental organizations. In recent years, providing NGOs with the National Intelligence Council's occasional estimates of anticipated complex humanitarian needs, for example, created a virtuous cycle of collaboration: NGOs became more familiar with government analysts and were motivated to share their data and perspectives on broad trends and patterns, which were then reflected in subsequent government reports.[15] These National Intelligence Council reports and other strategic trend analyses, to be sure, serve only a small portion of the NGO community; however, since they go to those responsible for planning and those in leadership positions, their influence is greater than the numbers suggest. In any event, such strategic information would be of less value to operational personnel who are the ones to deploy to emergency situations.

Since the early 1990s, the UN has become more active in running or supporting peace-moni-

---

[15] The National Intelligence Council (NIC) produced these assessments roughly every 18 months in the mid-to-late-1990s. The two most recent assessments, both titled *Global Humanitarian Emergencies: Trends and Projections,* were published in 1999 and 2001. They can be found on the NIC's homepage at http://www.odci. gov/nic.

toring operations. The end of the Cold War stimulated the resolution of some longstanding conflicts in the Third World and a number of conflicts that erupted in the 1990s have been resolved.[16] The demand for information to support peace operations—which range from military forces monitoring cease-fires and keeping former enemies separated to peace-building, with its focus on rule of law and transitional justice programs—remains strong. US intelligence has aided peace operations through information-sharing at UN headquarters, in the field, and at war crimes tribunals in Africa and Europe.

These sustained information-sharing relationships required the development of a formal process to determine what information is available, what can be declassified, and what can be shared on a timely basis. Internal intelligence community agreements, called Concepts of Operations (ConOps), are used to set forth the appropriate procedures. They usually identify a lead agency to manage the ConOps and can be bound by the duration of a particular crisis or task. At present there are about two dozen ConOps in effect.

The careful interagency process that produces ConOps for sharing does not ensure that the

---

[16] At its peak, there were over 20 UN-led peace operations with 80,000 personnel. Today there are 66,000 personnel (including 15,000 civilians) deployed in 18 UN peace operations around the world.

> ## "
> ## Analysts concede that reporting from NGOs is of growing value.
> ## "

information will be useful to the operation. It is sometimes the case that what is shared is determined by what is available at low risk to US interests, rather than by the needs of the other party. As a result, some in the international community and in the NGO world have lost interest in formal sharing arrangements. They have complained that what the US government shares is usually what has already been in the news. Despite efforts to create timely mechanisms for sanitizing intelligence documents, what is released is often based on the previous day's reporting and may indeed be behind the curve in the CNN-driven information marketplace.

A New Equation

The information age has set new records for the sheer volume and speed with which information is available to all, with no geographic boundaries. The quantity of information on all conceivable topics, however, says little about the quality or reliability of that data. Responsible people in information-dependent professions would quickly eschew the notion that the Internet can make everyone an expert on a topic of their choice. Professional information processors are still important, given that information must be selected, assessed, and corroborated before being used for decisionmaking. Under these circumstances, intelligence professionals have become, or should be, valued for their meth-

odological rigor as much as for the secrets they provide.[17]

Nonetheless, exchanges with NGO officials who manage or directly conduct field operations around the world suggest that their organizations have modest expectations about mutually beneficial information-sharing with the US government. At the same time, government analysts concede that reporting available electronically or through direct contact with various NGOs is of considerable and growing value in monitoring and understanding many post-conflict situations where a US presence is limited or lacking.

While NGOs may press less often for information from government, the trend of interdependence between NGOs and government organizations supporting or engaging in post-conflict peace operations is on the rise. NGOs and government groups are partners in many situations, whether they recognize it in capitals or not. In fact, the relationships established in the mid-1990s in the Balkans and more recently in Afghanistan have led to closer ties through a new phenomenon: Large numbers of former military officers, former

ambassadors, and retired government officials have moved into the NGO sector to help promote development and humanitarian relief. These individuals bring their knowledge of government connections with them, which facilitates information-sharing.

Intelligence community reform provides a useful moment to reflect on information-sharing policies and whether they can be improved. The mega-message of the recent reports critical of intelligence performance is to share, not hoard, information. The most recent report on intelligence and Iraqi weapons of mass destruction addresses at length the need to integrate information, rather than use it in bureaucratic competitions.[18] The spirit, therefore, of intelligence reform would suggest a more flexible approach to sharing and a greater awareness of the benefits to US security when sharing takes place.

But several caveats come to mind. First, the reports are mostly concerned about sharing *within* the US government, not with outside parties. They are focused on the sharing of secret information that must remain secret to deter and disrupt hostile acts against US interests. It is not commonly believed within the Intelligence Community that

---

[17] In fact, the ratio of secrets to open information is changing rapidly. Intelligence leaders readily acknowledge in public testimony that an overwhelming portion of current analysis is now based on unclassified information.

[18] The Commission on the Intelligence Capabilities of the United States regarding Weapons of Mass Destruction, *Report to the President of the United States* (Washington: Government Printing Office, 31 March 2005). Also available on line at: http://www.wmd.gov.

> **" This moment of change in the intelligence business is an opportunity to modernize relationships with NGOs. "**

sharing with nongovernmental organizations would advance these objectives—although the proposition is worthy of debate.

Second, the impulse for intelligence reform is now being carried out in the context of new legislation in which the Director of National Intelligence is expected to be a stronger manager of the intelligence agencies than was the case with the Director of Central Intelligence under the predecessor system. This implies a desire for greater centralization. With respect to information-sharing with NGOs, however, sometimes what is needed is more autonomy and authority for the individual agencies, which may enable discrete sharing with NGOs of benefit to both parties. This has worked well for the State Department's Bureau of Intelligence and Research, with its relatively easy access to diplomatic exchanges and its proximity to AID, and the Defense Intelligence Agency, which directly supports US armed forces in peace operations.

If implemented, some of the recommendations of the WMD report may provide a silver lining. If security procedures and personnel security clearances are streamlined and simplified, and if originator-controlled systems are revised so that the government as a whole, not individual agencies, controls information, then sharing is likely to be greatly facilitated. Agencies would be on stronger ground and have clearer guidelines with respect to sharing

by having a common classification system—they would not have to go through complex bureaucratic exercises to obtain permission to share. In a best case scenario, once a policy determination is made, the development of a ConOp for sharing would be a simpler task and sharing could commence earlier in the life-cycle of a crisis.

In Sum

The dramatic changes in information technology and the nearly universal availability of Web-based information systems have empowered NGOs and freed them from heavy reliance on government to do their jobs. Ironically, NGOs have also mushroomed in part because government has been willing to fund them to perform services and tasks that might otherwise be implemented by soldiers and civil servants. Thus, the interdependence of the official world of government and the "third sector" is growing, and information needs to be part of the equation.

NGOs and government interlocutors need to learn to communicate more clearly. Usually, NGOs seek practical information and are not focused on whether it is classified. If relationships are established,

experienced officers can interpret the requests and determine whether information can be provided at no risk or low risk to intelligence equities. At the same time, government officers need to be more sensitive and respectful of boundaries when seeking information from NGOs. Most of the time, there is a shared sense of purpose, but players on both sides can lose that focus under the stress of trying to respond to a fast-changing crisis.

Information-sharing is part of a larger story—of the rise of NGOs and their growing competence; of the need for a reform of intelligence culture, so that government analysts are rewarded for integrating all available source material into their work and engaging with nongovernment experts; and of globalization, where agile partnerships between formal state structures and civil society are constantly emerging. The need to share is recognized by government and NGOs—it already occurs in many places between professionals who have learned to cross the cultural divide. Greater awareness of what NGOs have to offer and ways in which government could share data more effectively at relatively low cost (in terms of time and security risk) would be a modest, but valuable, contribution to post-conflict engagements. This moment of change in the intelligence business is an opportunity to improve information-sharing and to modernize an increasingly important set of relationships.

Developing an Intelligence Capability

João Vaz Antunes

"

The 'pilgrims' of the EU security architecture realized that . . . intelligence capabilities are a prerequisite for mission accomplishment.

"

Portuguese **Maj. Gen. João Nuno Jorge Vaz Antunes** directs the European Union Military Staff's Intelligence Division.

Of all the prerogatives of states, security and defence policy is probably the one which least lends itself to a collective European approach; however, after the single currency, it is in this dimension that the Union has made the most rapid and spectacular progress over the last five years.

—Secretary General/High Representative Dr. Javier Solana[1]

Today, a European security and defense policy is not a vision, but a reality. In only a few years and at breathtaking speed, the European Union (EU) has put in place not only the conceptual framework for a new security strategy but also the instruments to deal with present challenges. Political and military committees are an expression of this development, as is the EU Military Staff.

The "pilgrims" of this architecture realized from the very beginning that functioning intelligence capabilities are a prerequisite for mission accomplishment. The EU Military Staff's Intelligence Division is recognized as *one of the instruments within an EU Intelli-*

---

[1] Preface to *EU Security and Defence Policy–The First Five Years (1999–2004)* (Paris: Institute for Strategic Studies, 2004).

gence Community, bringing together various sources such as civilian services; law enforcement and police authorities; diplomatic, economic, and political reporting; and, last but not least, what could be labeled "military intelligence." From the start, the Intelligence Division has proactively pursued close cooperation and coordination with other EU early warning bodies, thus contributing to intelligence products needed for EU decisionmaking. It will remain a feature and strength of the European Union that it is the only multinational organization with economic, commercial, humanitarian, political, diplomatic, and military resources at its disposal. This multifaceted approach finds its reflection in the way the EU is dealing with intelligence requirements.

The Intelligence Division depends on EU member states and their defense intelligence organizations. The procedures in place allow for close cooperation with member states and day-to-day coordination among EU early warning bodies. As Europe's security and defense policy develops further and structures and procedures are adapted to new circumstances and challenges, such close cooperation will become even more salient. The Division has found its place in

---

> ## " The procedures in place allow for day-to-day coordination among EU early warning bodies. "

Origins

The EU General Secretariat's main building in Brussels—the Justus Lipsius Building, located opposite the well-known Berlaymont and Charlemagne Buildings at the Schuman traffic circle—still holds some surprises for its visitors and employees. One of them is spotting colorful uniforms among the many business-suited people in the hallways and meeting rooms. Inevitably questions arise as to the reason for the presence of military officers within the EU environment. While some assume the uniformed individuals are "politically interested visitors," they would, if asked, introduce themselves as members of the European Union Military Staff, working for Dr. Javier Solana on military matters related to European security and defense policy.

Three compelling political factors have fueled the relatively rapid development of an EU security and defense policy. First, a growing number of crises and situations of international instability have arisen in the EU's strategic environment, both in its neighborhood and in more distant parts of the world. Second, in a globalized, chaotic world, it is no longer possible to artificially separate prosperity and security. The economic and com-

mercial influence now achieved by the EU's 25 members—which account for a quarter of the world's GNP and 450 million inhabitants—and the closer integration of their economies means that Europe can no longer stand comfortably aside from the world's convulsions or evade its political responsibilities. Finally, the EU's framework makes multilateralism logical and unavoidable in the management of international crises.

The decision by the Cologne European Council in June 1999 "to give the European Union the necessary means and capabilities to assume its responsibilities regarding a Common European Policy on Security and Defence" marked the starting point of an entirely new chapter in European history.[2] Indeed, the EU Security and Defence Policy of today is no longer a vision but a reality, as are its instruments, such as the new committees—namely, the Political and Security Committee, the Civil Committee, and the European Union Military Committee—and the new elements of the EU Council General Secretariat, such as the EU Policy Unit,[3]

---

[2] It was also at the Cologne Council meeting that Dr. Solana was appointed the first Secretary General/High Representative for the Common Foreign and Security Policy.

the Joint Situation Center, and the EU Military Staff, located just three blocks away from the Justus Lipsius Building on Corthenberg Avenue, Brussels.

A Distinct Departure

The establishment of the Military Staff within the EU structure marked the introduction of a military facet into what was formerly considered a strictly politico-diplomatic-economic organization. Notwithstanding the fact that EU members had clearly endorsed the introduction of a security policy into the overall EU framework and the establishment of the necessary staff elements, it took some time until the visible military presence within EU premises was taken for granted and the need for military advice and contributions in an overall EU crisis management process was fully acknowledged by all EU actors.

From the very beginning, the Military Staff has been looked at as but *one* instrument in an orchestrated, multifaceted approach to security policy. Members of the Staff, seconded by EU member states, quickly came to consider themselves as part of an EU team, consisting of civilian, police, and military personnel, all working closely together to make security policy a reality. The full establishment of the Military Staff took about a year, after a

---

[3] The full title being the Policy Planning and Early Warning Unit of the High Representative for Common Foreign and Security Policy.

short build-up period in 2001. During that time, decisions were made regarding such complex internal activities as designing infrastructure and information technology, managing the influx of personnel, overseeing working conditions, and developing internal training.

By 2003, a common basis for EU-led crisis management operations had been laid. That year saw four EU operations launched: the EU Police Mission in Bosnia and Herzegovina; Operation CONCORDIA in the former Yugoslavia; Operation ARTEMIS in the Democratic Republic of Congo; and a second Police Mission, PROXIMA, in the Balkans. In July 2004, EUJUST THEMIS in Georgia represented the first EU rule-of-law mission in the context of European defense policy. And, finally, the transfer of authority from NATO-led forces to EU Operation ALTHEA in Bosnia and Herzegovina in December 2004 marked another major step in the evolution of European security policy. The EU Military Staff was a major player in the planning and coordination of these actions, especially Operations CONCORDIA, ARTEMIS, and ALTHEA.

Mission and Structure

Based on decisions of the December 1999 Helsinki European Council, the EU Military Staff provides military expertise and support for the implementation of security and defense policy, including the conduct of EU-led

> ❝
> **Given the complexity of crisis management, the EU Military Staff is astonishingly small.**
> ❞

military crisis management operations. To this end, the Staff performs three tasks: early warning, situation assessment, and strategic planning.

As an integral element of the EU Council General Secretariat, the Military Staff is labeled a "General Directorate" and is headed by a "Director General" (DG) who is a three-star flag officer. The DG reports to the Secretary General/High Representative, Dr. Solana. At the same time, the Staff is what can be considered the "working muscle" of the European Union Military Committee, comprising the permanent representatives of the chiefs of defense of the 25 EU member states.[4]

It is important to note that the Military Staff has no subordinate standing headquarters to carry out any of its tasks. Instead, the EU crisis management procedures foresee a number of so-called "operations headquarters" that could be activated on the basis of an EU Council decision, if needed. For this purpose, five EU members have offered national headquarters, which would turn into multinational EU operations

_____

[4] Most of the EU member states' military representatives on the EU Military Committee are "double-hatted," representing their chiefs of defense also on the NATO Military Committee.

headquarters for a particular EU-led crisis management operation.[5] Likewise, lower echelon staffs, such as force headquarters, would be allocated to member states as an EU crisis management process proceeds. In the particular case of an EU-led crisis management operation with recourse to NATO assets and capabilities, SHAPE at Mons/Belgium is the designated EU operations headquarters.[6]

Every now and then, people argue that the EU's organization is cumbersome, difficult to understand, and—at any rate–overstaffed. This is not quite right with regard to the Military Staff. The Staff was originally structured along classical military lines, with a director at three-star flag rank, a two-star deputy serving as chief of staff, and five divisions, each headed by a one-star director. The five divisions are: Policy and Plans; Intelligence; Operations and Exercises; Logistics and Resources; and Communications, Information, and Security.

Given the range of tasks allocated, the number of EU agencies and organizations to coordinate with, and the complexity of the EU crisis management decision

_____

[5] France, Germany, Greece, Italy, and the UK. Operation ARTEMIS, for example, was conducted by an EU operations headquarters in Paris.
[6] This was successfully exercised in Operation CONCORDIA. An even more challenging operation for the EU operations headquarters at SHAPE commenced in December 2004 with the transfer of authority from NATO to EU Operation ALTHEA in Bosnia and Herzegovina.

> ## " The Intelligence Division does not have its own collection capabilities. "

process, the Military Staff is run by an astonishingly small number of people. Some 140 peacetime posts were approved by the member states, the providers of the personnel. These officers carry out a growing number of tasks in an increasingly visible EU security and defense policy environment. One of the greatest challenges, and a key feature of the Staff's work, is the requirement to coordinate and cooperate on a daily basis with civilian colleagues from other EU bodies. It cannot be emphasized enough that it is this unique mix of civilian and military capabilities that makes the difference between the European Union and other multinational organizations, and that constitutes the added value of EU security and defense policy activities.

The Intelligence Division

Common threat assessments are the best basis for common action. This requires improved sharing of intelligence among Member States and with partners.[7]

The Intelligence Division, comprising 33 individuals from 19 member states, is the largest component of the EU Military Staff, reflecting its tasks and particular working procedures. It will come as no surprise that the Military Staff's Intelligence Division follows a classic organizational pat-

---

[7] From "A Secure Europe in a Better World," the European security strategy adopted by EU heads of state and government at the Brussels European Council, 12 December 2003.

tern. Its three branches—Policy, Requirements, and Production—are led by full colonels. As a rule, positions of branch chief and above are "non-quota posts," eligible to be filled by any member state on a three-year-turnover basis. Positions of action officers and non-commissioned officers are "quota posts," allocated to respective member states.

Intelligence Policy Branch—Develops intelligence-related concepts, doctrines, and procedures, in coordination with relevant civilian EU bodies, and manages intelligence-related personnel, infrastructure, and communications matters. For crisis management procedures and EU-led operations, the Policy Branch creates appropriate intelligence architecture and procedures. For EU exercises, it prepares scenarios and intelligence specifications. It is responsible for coordinating the Intelligence Division's contributions in support of other Military Staff elements. The Policy Branch also organizes the Military Staff's Intelligence Directors Conclave, an annual informal exchange on EU intelligence matters between the directors of defense intelligence organizations in the member states and the EU Military Staff.

Requirements Branch—Fosters the relationship with EU mem-

ber states' defense intelligence organizations, including arranging regular bilateral meetings and maintaining a system of points-of-contact to ensure direct links with member intelligence organizations. The Requirements Branch handles the distribution of requests for information. It also coordinates with the EU satellite center at Torrejon, Spain, and develops Military Staff inputs for the EU ISTAR (Intelligence, Surveillance, Target Acquisition, and Reconnaissance) process.

Production Branch—Develops the classified "EU Watchlist" in coordination with other EU early warning bodies, such as the Policy Unit, the Joint Situation Center, and the EU Commission. Updated on a regular basis, the Watchlist focuses on areas or issues of security concern. It is adopted by the Political and Security Committee. The Watchlist constitutes the common basis for intelligence exchanges with member states' defense intelligence organizations. The Production Branch is organized into five task forces covering specific geographic regions and one task force for transnational issues. It contributes to all-source situation assessments, in cooperation mainly with the Joint Situation Center, and also produces regular intelligence briefs for the Military Staff and "on-the-spot" intelligence assessments for the Military Staff, the Military Committee, and the Secretary General.

Relations with Member States

Similar to other multinational military organizations, the EU Intelligence Division does not have its own collection capabilities—with the exception of the aforementioned EU Satellite Center—and depends almost entirely on member states' intelligence contributions. This dependence parallels EU structures as a whole.

The Division's three main tasks—early warning, situation assessment, and strategic planning—can only be carried out appropriately if and when timely and comprehensive intelligence is available. The founders of the Intelligence Division quickly realized that it would take a particular type of relationship between the Military Staff and member states' defense intelligence organizations and particular procedures for EU intelligence production to meet this requirement.

The Intelligence Division works on strengthening critically needed collaboration in four ways:

First, the Division maintains strong links with national defense intelligence organizations through regular updates of what intelligence is required in terms of regions, issues, and timelines. Visits to capitals and, in turn, bilateral meetings in Brussels with member-state representatives support the development of a mutual understanding of EU Military Staff require-

> **" The EU Watchlist enables continuous dialog with members' intelligence organizations. "**

ments, on the one hand, and the strengths (and sometimes limitations) of members' organizations, on the other hand. In this context, the EU Watchlist is a useful tool. The continuous dialog on Watchlist matters enables the EU Military Staff to submit requests for information on a case-by-case basis to those defense intelligence organizations that can contribute to a particular intelligence product.

Second, the Intelligence Division has refined its points-of-contact system so that officers seconded by member states and filling intelligence analyst posts for particular regions or subjects act in a secondary function as interfaces with (and representatives of) their home organizations, maintaining secure communication links to their parent services. This arrangement facilitates "on the spot" coordination, resulting in more responsive and precise intelligence products for EU purposes.

Third, taking into account the experiences of other multinational organizations, the Division never tries to produce "EU agreed intelligence products." The Military Staff receives finished intelligence from members' defense intelligence organizations, which are marked releasable to the EU. The Production Branch then uses

these inputs, without any reference to sources, for the development of its own intelligence products, labeled "EU Military Staff Intelligence Division," thereby taking full responsibility for their contents and conclusions. The same rule applies to the Division's contributions to the Joint Situation Center's all-source situation assessments. All finalized EU intelligence products are, in turn, sent to member defense intelligence organizations for their information.

Fourth, the Division cooperates daily with civilian early warning bodies, ensuring that the requirement of a comprehensive, "joint" intelligence approach is met. Information available at the Joint Situation Center, the Policy Unit, and the EU Commission makes for quite a heterogeneous information picture, which is supplemented by "military intelligence." Merging all these pieces of information into comprehensive and sound intelligence products is a considerable challenge. Apart from its role as a proactive player in the EU Intelligence Community, the Intelligence Division holds sole responsibility for assessments of the security situation in a given country or region. Especially in the event of an emerging crisis or an EU-led crisis management operation with a military component, the Military Staff carries the primary responsibility for assessing the risks and their implications for force and mission protection.

> ## " The Division is recognized as expert in security issues. "

The Way Ahead

Only five years old, the EU security and defense policy is still just beginning. Crisis management activities are complex in nature and, in most cases, require the use of both civilian *and* military means and capabilities. As stated earlier, it is exactly this mix that makes the EU role in crisis management so unique. The European Council in December 2003 directed the Council General Secretariat to "enhance the capacity of the [Military Staff] to conduct early warning, situation assessment, and strategic planning through the establishment . . . of a cell with civil/military components." This new civil/military cell, established in the summer of 2005 as an additional division of the EU Military Staff, is headed by a one-star flag officer with a civilian deputy and comprises some 30 military and civilian personnel. Beside its strategic tasks—contingency planning and crisis response planning—the cell provides temporary reinforcement to national operations headquarters and support for the generation of an EU operations center when needed to oversee

autonomous EU operations, in particular when a joint civilian-military response is required and no national headquarters has been identified. The civil/military cell is slated to include one intelligence planner, and the operations center is to have a limited, but self-sustainable, intelligence working element, provided by both the EU Intelligence Division ("double-hatted") and member states. The new cell and the operations center, when activated, will constitute additional recipients for EU intelligence products.

It goes without saying that the intelligence element in the new civil/military cell will rely heavily on the expertise and manpower of the EU Intelligence Division. In this regard, current relations with other Military Staff divisions will not significantly alter; however, they will become more focused on this "new" division. It remains to be seen what impact staffing demands will have on the remaining Division personnel still fulfilling "regular" staff work and tasks beyond crisis management operations.

Clearly, cooperation and coordination among the various EU early warning bodies is likely to become even more important. Indeed, the Intelligence Division is determined to work to this end, bringing its own expertise even closer together with the significant capabilities available to the Joint Situation Center, the Policy Unit, and especially the EU Commission. The latter has considerable information gathering capabilities, mainly through its comprehensive open-source exploitation mechanism. In addition, the EU Commission is a main addressee of frequent and substantial situation reporting provided by its mission delegations around the globe.

So far, the EU Intelligence Division has not done badly and has developed a recognized standing as an expert on military and security issues. It remains a challenge, however, to develop EU intelligence capabilities further in order to meet the challenges of tomorrow's problems.

Creation of a National Institute for Analytic Methods

Steven Rieber and Neil Thomason

> *Traditionally, analysts at all levels devote little attention to improving how they think. To penetrate the heart and soul of the problem of improving analysis, it is necessary to better understand, influence, and guide the mental processes of analysts themselves.*
>
> —Richards J. Heuer, Jr.[1]

“ The opinions of experts regarding which methods work may be misleading or seriously wrong. ”

The United States needs to improve its capacity to deliver timely, accurate intelligence. Recent commission reports have made various proposals aimed at achieving this goal. These recommendations are based on many months of careful deliberation by highly experienced experts and are intuitively plausible. However, a considerable body of evidence from a wide range of fields indicates that the opinions of experts regarding which methods work may be misleading or seriously wrong. Better analysis requires independent scientific research. To carry out this research, the United States should establish a National Institute for Analytic Methods, analogous to the National Institutes of Health.

While much has been written about how to improve intelligence analysis, this article will show *how to improve the process of improving analysis*. The key is to conduct scientific research to determine what works and what does not, and then to ensure that the Intelligence Community uses the results of this research. [2]

Expert Opinions Can Be Unreliable

The reports of recent commissions examining the intelligence process—including the Senate Select Committee on Intelligence and the special presidential commission on Iraq weapons of mass destruction[3]—incorporate recommendations for improving analysis. These proposals, which include establishing a center for analyzing open-source intelli-

Steven Rieber is a scholar-in-residence at the CIA's Kent Center for Analytic Tradecraft. **Neil Thomason** is a senior lecturer in history and philosophy of science at the University of Melbourne. This paper is an extract of a longer manuscript in progress.

[1] *Psychology of Intelligence Analysis* (Washington: CIA Center for the Study of Intelligence, 1999), 173.

[2] Steven Rieber would like to express his deep appreciation to the Kent Center for Analytic Tradecraft for providing a stimulating environment for thought and discussion. The opinions expressed here are the authors' alone.

[3] *Report of the Senate Select Committee on Intelligence on the US Intelligence Community's Prewar Intelligence Assessments on Iraq*, 7 July 2004, and *The Commission on the Intelligence Capabilities of the United States Regarding Weapons of Mass Destruction Report to the President of the United States* [hereafter *WMD Commission Report*], 31 March 2005.

> ## " The only way to test conventional wisdom is to conduct rigorous scientific studies. "

gence and creating "mission managers" for specific intelligence problems, make intuitive sense.

We want to suggest, however, that this intuitive approach to improving intelligence analysis is insufficient. Examples from a wide range of fields show that experts' opinions about which methods work are often dead wrong:

• For decades, steroids have been the standard treatment for head-injury patients. This treatment "makes sense" because head trauma results in swelling and steroids reduce swelling. However, a recent meta-analysis involving over 10,000 patients shows that giving steroids to head-injury patients apparently increases mortality.[4]

• Most police departments make identifications by showing an eyewitness six photos of possible suspects simultaneously. However, a series of experiments has demonstrated that presenting the photos sequentially, rather than simultaneously, substantially improves accuracy.[5]

• The nation's most popular anti-drug program for school-age children, DARE (Drug Abuse Resistance Education), brings

police officers into classrooms to teach about substance abuse and decisionmaking and to boost students' self-esteem. But two randomized controlled trials involving nearly 9,000 students have shown that DARE has no significant effect on students' use of cigarettes, alcohol, or illicit drugs.[6]

• Baseball scouting typically is done intuitively, using a traditional set of statistics such as batting average. Scouts and managers believe that they can ascertain a player's potential by looking at the statistics and watching him play. However, their intuitions are not very good and many of the common statistical measures are far from ideal. Sophisticated statistical analysis reveals that batting average is a substan-

tially less accurate predictor of whether a batter will score than on-base percentage, which includes walks. The Oakland A's were the first team to use the new statistical techniques to dramatically improve their performance despite an annual budget far smaller than those of most other teams.[7]

These examples and many others illustrate two important points. First, even sincere, well-informed experts with many years of collective experience are often mistaken about what are the best methods. Second, the only way to determine whether the conventional wisdom is right is to conduct rigorous scientific studies using careful measurement and statistical analysis. Prior to the meta-analysis on the effects of steroids, there was no way of knowing that they were counterproductive for head injuries. And without randomized controlled studies, we would not have learned that DARE fails to reduce cigarette, drug, and alcohol use. Experts' intuitive beliefs about what works are not only frequently wrong, but also are generally not self-correcting.

Caution Advised

Consequently, we should be skeptical about the numerous recent proposals for improving intelligence analysis. The recommendations generally are based on years of

---

[4] CRASH Trial Collaborators, "Effect of Intravenous Corticosteroids on Death Within 14 days in 10008 Adults with Clinically Significant Head Injury (MRC CRASH Trial): Randomized Placebo-Controlled Trial," *Lancet* 364 (2004): 1321–28.

[5] Gary L. Wells and Elizabeth A. Olson, "Eyewitness Testimony," *Annual Review of Psychology* 54 (2003): 277–95. For an illuminating account of the damage caused by ongoing institutional resistance to evidence-based reform of eyewitness practices, see Atul Gawande. "Under Suspicion: The Fugitive Science of Criminal Justice," *New Yorker,* 8 January 2001: 50–53.

[6] Cheryl L. Perry, Kelli A. Komro, Sara Veblen-Mortenson, Linda M. Bosma, Kian Farbakhsh, Karen A. Munson, Melissa H. Stigler, and Leslie A. Lytle, "A Randomized Controlled Trial of the Middle and Junior High School D.A.R.E. and D.A.R.E. Plus Programs," *Archives of Pediatric and Adolescent Medicine* 157 (2003): 178–84.

[7] Michael Lewis, *Moneyball* (New York: Norton, 2003).

> **The research on devil's advocacy is quite equivocal.**

experience, deep familiarity with the problems, careful reflection, and a sincere desire to help—all of which may lead to reforms that do as much harm as good. Some of the experts' sincere beliefs may be correct; others may be widely off the mark. Without systematic research, it is impossible to tell.

Some high-quality research relevant to intelligence analysis has already been done, but it is virtually unknown within the Intelligence Community. Consider, for example, devil's advocacy. Both the Senate report on Iraq's weapons of mass destruction (WMD) and the report of the president's commission proposed the use of devil's advocates.[8] In fact, devil's advocacy and "red teams"—which construct and press an alternate interpretation of how events might evolve or how information might be interpreted—are the only specific analytic techniques recommended by the Senate report, the president's commission report, and the 2004 Intelligence Reform Act.[9] None of these reports, however, mentions the research on devil's advocacy, which is quite equivocal about whether this technique improves group judgment.[10] Some research suggests that devil's advocates may even aggravate groupthink (the tendency of group members

to suppress their doubts).[11] As Charlan Nemeth writes:

> . . . the results . . . showed a negative, unintended consequence of devil's advocate. The [devil's advocate] stimulated significantly more thoughts in support of the initial position. Thus subjects appeared to generate new ideas aimed at cognitive bolstering of their initial viewpoint but they did not generate thoughts regarding other positions. . . .[12]

Irving Janis, the author of *Groupthink*, suggested such possibilities over 30 years ago. Janis describes the use of devil's advocates by President Lyndon B. Johnson's administration:

> [Stanford political scientist] Alexander George also comments that, paradoxically, the institutionalized devil's advocate, instead of stirring up much-needed turbulence among the members of a policy-making group, may create 'the comforting feeling that they have considered all sides of the issue and that the policy chosen has weathered challenges from within the decision-making circle.' He goes on to say that after the President has fostered the ritualized use of devil's advocates, the top-level officials may learn nothing more than how to enact their policy-making in such a way as to meet the informed public's expectation about how important decisions should be made and 'to project a favorable image into the instant histories that will be written shortly thereafter.'[13]

Thus, once institutionalized, the principal effect of devil's advocates may be to protect the Intelligence Community from future criticism and calls for reform. The scientific evidence shows that we cannot exclude the possibility that adopting the recommendations of the recent

---

8 *Report of the Senate Select Committee on Intelligence*, 21, and *WMD Commission Report*, 407.

9 *House Report 108-796, Intelligence Reform and Terrorism Prevention Act of 2004*, Conference Report to Accompany 2845, 108th cong., 2nd sess., 35.

10 Gary Katzenstein, "The Debate on Structured Debate: Toward a Unified Theory," *Organizational Behavior and Human Decision Processes* 66 (1996): 316–32; Alexander L. George and Eric K. Stern, "Harnessing Conflict in Foreign Policy Making: From Devil's to Multiple Advocacy," *Presidential Studies Quarterly* 32 (2002): 484–508.

11 While it is certainly true that groups sometimes suppress their doubts, there is considerable debate over the mechanisms of such suppression. Many people mistakenly identify all suppression of doubts with groupthink: "The unconditional acceptance of the groupthink phenomenon without due regard for the body of scientific evidence surrounding it leads to unthinking conformity to a theoretical standpoint that may be invalid for the majority of circumstances." Marlene E. Turner and Anthony R. Pratkinis, "Twenty-Five Years of Groupthink Theory and Research: Lessons from the Evaluation of a Theory," *Organizational Behavior and Human Decision Processes* 73 (1998): 105–15

12 Charlan Nemeth, Keith Brown, and John Rogers, "Devil's Advocate vs. Authentic Dissent: Stimulating Quantity and Quality," *European Journal of Social Psychology* 31 (2001): 707–20.

13 Irving L. Janis, *Groupthink: Psychological Studies of Policy Decisions and Fiascoes*, 2nd ed. (Boston: Houghton Mifflin, 1982), 268.

commission reports may be counterproductive.

Identifying What the Research Says

The first element in improving the process of improving analysis is to *find out what the existing scientific research says.* Not all of the existing research on how to improve human judgment is negative. Here are some promising results from this research:

• Argument mapping, a technique for visually displaying an argument's logical structure and evidence, substantially enhances critical thinking abilities.[14]

• Systematic feedback on accuracy makes judgments more accurate.[15]

• There are effective methods to help people easily avoid the omnipresent and serious fallacy of base-rate neglect.[16]

• Combining distinct forecasts by averaging usually raises accuracy, sometimes substantially.[17]

> ❝
> **Not all research on improving human judgment is negative.**
> ❞

• Consulting a statistical model generally increases the accuracy of expert forecasts.[18]

• A certain cognitive style, marked by open-mindedness and skepticism toward grand theories, is associated with substantially better judgments about international affairs.[19]

• Simulated interactions (a type of structured role-playing) yields forecasts about conflict situations that are much more accurate than those produced by unaided judgments or by game theory.[20]

Applying the Research to Intelligence

While each of these findings is promising, almost none of this research has been conducted on analysts working on intelligence problems. Thus, the second element of improving the process of improving analysis is to *initiate systematic research on promising methods for improving analysis.*[21]

Each of the analytic methods mentioned above suggests numerous lines of research. In the case of argument mapping, for example, questions that should be investigated include: Do argument maps improve analytic judgment? In which domains (political, economic, military, long-range, or short-range forecasts) are argument maps most effective? How can analysts be encouraged to use the results of argument mapping in their written products? How can this method be effectively taught? If devil's advocates use argument maps, will their objections be taken more seriously?

The only reliable way to answer each of these questions is through scientific studies carefully designed to measure the relevant factors, control for extraneous

---

14 Tim van Gelder, Melanie Bissett, and Geoff Cumming, "Cultivating Expertise in Informal Reasoning," *Canadian Journal of Experimental Psychology* 58 (2004): 142–52.

15 Fergus Bolger and George Wright, "Assessing the Quality of Expert Judgment," *Decision Support Systems* 11 (1994): 1–24.

16 Peter Sedlmeier and Gerd Gigerenzer, "Teaching Bayesian Reasoning in Less Than Two Hours," *Journal of Experimental Psychology: General* 130 (2001): 380–400.

17 J. Scott Armstrong, "Combining Forecasts," in J. Scott Armstrong, ed., *Principles of Forecasting* (Boston, MA: Kluwer, 2001), 417–39.

18 William M. Grove, David H. Zald, Boyd S. Lebow, Beth E. Snitz, and Chad Nelson, "Clinical Versus Mechanical Prediction: A Meta-Analysis," *Psychological Assessment* 12 (2000): 19–30; John A. Swets, Robyn M. Dawes, and John Monahan, "Psychological Science Can Improve Diagnostic Decisions," *Psychological Science in the Public Interest* 1 (2000): 1–26.

19 Philip E. Tetlock, *Expert Political Judgment: How Good Is It? How Can We Know?* (Princeton, NJ: Princeton University Press, 2005.)

20 Kesten C. Green, "Forecasting Decisions in Conflict Situations: A Comparison of Game Theory, Role-playing, and Unaided Judgement," *International Journal of Forecasting* 18 (2002): 321–44.

21 Two examples of this type of research are: Robert D. Folker, Jr., "Exploiting Structured Methodologies to Improve Qualitative Intelligence Analysis," unpublished masters thesis, Joint Military Intelligence College (1999); and Brant A. Cheikes, Mark J. Brown, Paul E. Lehner, and Leonard Adelman, "Confirmation Bias in Complex Analysis," MITRE Technical Report MTR 04B0000017 (2004).

---

influences, distinguish causation from correlation, and produce sizable effects. Intelligence analysts and other experts will certainly have opinions about how best to employ argument maps; in some cases, the experts may even agree with one another. But while the expert opinions should be considered in designing the research, they should not be the last word, since they may be mistaken.

Evaluation and development should be ongoing and concurrent and should provide feedback to the next round of evaluation and development, in a spiraling process. Evaluation results will suggest ways of refining promising techniques, and the refined techniques can then be assessed.

Encouraging Use of New Methods

It is essential that there be serious research both inside and outside the analysis sector itself. American universities can become one of our great security assets. Techniques for improving analytic judgment can be tested initially on university students (both undergraduate and graduate); promising methods can then be refined and tested further by contractors, including former analysts, with security clearances. Techniques that are easy to employ and that substantially increase accuracy in these preliminary stages of evaluation could then be tested with practicing analysts.

> ## " Evaluation and development should be ongoing and concurrent. "

It is essential to expose analysts only to methods that they are likely to use, and use well. Subjecting them to cumbersome or ineffective techniques would only waste their time and increase their possible skepticism about new methods.

Research should investigate not only which techniques improve analytic judgment, but also how to teach these techniques and how to get analysts to use them. Analytic methods that produce excellent results in the laboratory will be worthless if not used, and used correctly, by practicing analysts. Thus the third element of improving the process of improving analysis is to *conduct research on how to get promising analytic methods effectively taught and used.*

Communicating with Consumers

The purpose of intelligence analysis is to inform policymakers to help them make better decisions. Accuracy, relevance, and timeliness are not enough; intelligence analysis must effectively convey information to the consumer. No matter how cogently analysts reason, their work will fail in its purpose if it is not correctly understood by the consumer. Thus the fourth element of improving the process of improving analysis is to *conduct*

research on improving communication to policymakers.

How analysts should communicate their judgments to policymakers is yet another issue on which opinions are plentiful but systematic research is scarce. Some important questions here are:

- How can tacit assumptions be made explicit and clear? Can visual representations of reasoning, such as structured argumentation, usefully supplement prose and speech?

- How can the differences between analysts (or agencies) be communicated most effectively?

- What are the best ways for analysts to express judgments that disagree with the views of policymakers?

- Is the ubiquitous PowerPoint presentation a good way to present complex information? Or does it "dumb down" complex issues?[22]

- Forty years ago, Sherman Kent showed that different experts in international affairs had very different understandings of words like "probable" and "likely," and that these differences produced serious

---

[22] The Columbia space shuttle investigation concluded: "The Board views the endemic use of PowerPoint briefing slides instead of technical papers as an illustration of the problematic methods of technical communication at NASA." *Columbia Accident Investigation Board Report,* Vol. 1 (August 2003), 191.

miscommunication. How can this ongoing cause of miscommunication be alleviated?[23]

These questions can be systematically answered only through scientific research. Associated with each question is a cluster of research issues. Take, for instance, the question of how to communicate probability. Should analysts' probabilistic judgments be conveyed verbally, numerically, or through a combination of the two? If verbal expressions are used, should they be given common meanings across analysts and agencies? Or should analysts assign their own numerical equivalents (making them explicit in their finished intelligence)? Should probabilistic statements be avoided altogether in favor of a discussion of possible outcomes and the reasons for each?

A National Institute

As shown by examples from other fields, systematic research can dramatically improve longstanding practices. This sort of research should be done on all aspects of intelligence analysis, including analytic methods, training, and communication to policymakers. To be most useful, the research should be well

66
How should analysts communicate probability?
99

funded, coordinated, and held to the highest scientific standards. This requires an institutional structure. The National Institutes of Health provide an excellent model: NIH conducts its own research and funds research in medical centers and universities across the world.[24]

Just as NIH improves our nation's health, a National Institute for Analytic Methods (NIAM) would enhance its security. To ensure that NIAM research would be of unimpeachable scientific caliber, it should work closely with, but independently of, the Intelligence Community. In a similar vein, the president's WMD Commission recommends the establishment of one or more "sponsored research institutes":

We envision the establishment of at least one not-for-profit 'sponsored research institute' to serve as a critical window into outside expertise for the Intelligence Community. This sponsored research institute would be funded by the Intelligence Community, but would be largely independent of Community management.[25]

The Commission points out that "there must be outside thinking to challenge conventional wisdom, and this institute would provide both the distance from and the link to the Intelligence Community to provide a useful counterpoint to accepted views."[26] While the sponsored research institutes envisioned by the WMD Commission would tackle substantive issues, the NIAM would confront the equally important problems of developing, teaching, and promoting effective analytic methods.

To achieve this excellence and independence, a leadership team consisting of preeminent experts from inside and outside government is essential. Such a team is probably the only means to ensure that the research would be scientifically rigorous and adventurous, and that reform proposals would be truly evidence based. Many people mistakenly believe that they know how to do social-scientific research. However, this research is difficult, the methodology is complex and statistically sophisticated, and established results are often counter-intuitive. Only if guided by scientists of the highest caliber would evidence-based analytic methods advance as rapidly as their importance demands.

There are also political and bureaucratic reasons for having an expert leadership team. With-

---

[23] Sherman Kent, "Words of Estimative Probability," *Studies in Intelligence* 8 (1964): 49–65; David Budescu and Thomas Wallsten, "Processing Linguistic Probabilities: General Principles and Empirical Evidence," in Busemeyer, et al., eds., *Decision Making from a Cognitive Perspective* (New York: Academic Press, 1995).

[24] For a different view of the analogy between intelligence analysis and medicine see Stephen Marrin and Jonathan Clemente, "Improving Intelligence Analysis by Looking to the Medical Profession," *International Journal of Intelligence and Counterintelligence*, 18 (2005): 707–29.

[25] *WMD Commission Report*, 399.
[26] Ibid.

> ## " Evidence-based [intelligence] reforms would continue indefinitely. "

out the prestige, influence, and financial clout of such a panel, bureaucratic inertia might prevent evidence-based reforms from being adopted. Bureaucratic rigidity is likely to become particularly serious as the intense political pressure for intelligence community reform diminishes. Initiating, funding, and coordinating research on all aspects of intelligence analysis is a large set of tasks. To perform these well, NIAM's budget would have to be adequate. When the Institute is fully running, a budget of 1–2 percent of NIH's may be appropriate.

A National Institute for Analytic Methods would contribute to long-term intelligence reforms in an unusual way. Most reforms become institutionalized and, thereafter, are rarely reevaluated until a subsequent crisis occurs. NIAM's evidence-based reforms would be very different. Because science itself is a self-correcting process, NIAM-generated science would ensure that evidence-based reforms continue indefinitely. Thus, intelligence reforms would continue to improve analysts' effectiveness long after the current political urgency fades.

The Wolves at the Door: The True Story of America's Greatest Female Spy

By Judith L. Pearson. Guilford, CT: The Lyon Press, 2005. 324 pages.

Reviewed by Hayden B. Peake

British historian M. R. D. Foot called her an "indomitable agent with a 'brass foot.'"[1] Special Operations Executive (SOE) officer Philippe de Vomécourt wrote that he served in France with this "extraordinary woman . . . with a wooden leg."[2] French author Marcel Ruby said that she lost her leg in a riding accident.[3] Others had her losing a limb after falling under a tram.[4] Former CIA officer Harry Mahoney describes an OSS mission in which she parachuted behind enemy lines with her "wooden leg in her knapsack."[5] Author and former OSS officer Elizabeth McIntosh wrote that she landed in France by boat.[6] The Gestapo put her likeness on a wanted poster. The British made her a Member of the British Empire. The United States awarded her the Distinguished Service Cross "for extraordinary heroism in connection with military operations against the enemy," the only women to receive that medal for World War II service.[7]

If ever a career in intelligence cried out for a biography, Virginia Hall's qualifies. Yet, in the 60 years since World War II, most histories of OSS fail to mention her.[8] Parts of her intriguing career have emerged gradually in articles and memoirs as official records became available. In the process, she has become something of a legend. When the British and American World War II intelligence archives were finally released in the 1980s and 1990s, it became possible to clarify contradic-

[1] M. R. D. Foot, *SOE in France: An Account of the Work of the British Special Operations Executive in France 1940–1944* (London: HMSO, 2004 revised), 155.
[2] Philippe de Vomécourt, *An Army of Amateurs* (Garden City, NY: Doubleday & Company, 1961), 223.
[3] Marcel Ruby. *F. Section SOE: The Story of the Buckmaster Network* (London: Leo Cooper, 1988), 65.
[4] Liane Jones, *A Quiet Courage: Women Agents in the French Resistance* (New York: Bantam Press, 1990), 17.
[5] M. H. Mahoney and Marjorie Locke Mahoney, *Biographic Dictionary of Espionage* (San Francisco, CA: Austin & Winfield Publishers, 1998), 265.
[6] Elizabeth P. McIntosh, *Sisterhood of Spies: The Women of the OSS* (Annapolis, MD: Naval Institute Press, 1998), 147.
[7] Ibid., 149.
[8] See for example, R. Harris Smith, *OSS: The Secret History of America's First Central Intelligence Agency* (Berkeley: University of California Press, 1972), and Bradley F. Smith, *Three Shadow Warriors: OSS and the Origins of the CIA* (New York: Basic Books, 1983).

Hayden B. Peake is the curator of the CIA Historical Intelligence Collection.

All statements of fact, opinion, or analysis expressed in this article are those of the author. Nothing in the article should be construed as asserting or implying US government endorsement of an article's factual statements and interpretations.

tions and separate fact from fable. Author Judith Pearson has done that in *The Wolves at the Door*.

This fascinating story begins with Hall's origins in Baltimore where it soon became evident that she had no intention of heading down the road of life to housewife-dom. After a year at Barnard and another at Radcliffe, she was off to Europe in 1926 to finish her education at the Sorborne in Paris and the Konsularakademie in Vienna. Then came a series of frustrating attempts to join the Foreign Service. She did not do well in her first examination, so she decided to gain experience and try again while working for the State Department as a clerk overseas. It was while in Turkey, in December 1933, that she lost her lower leg in a hunting accident. After recovering at home, she was fitted with a wooden prosthesis that had rubber under the foot.[9] She then returned to her clerk duties, this time in Venice, Italy, where her foreign service dreams ended: She was told that Department regulations prohibited hiring anyone without the necessary number of appendages. Needing a fresh start, Hall transferred to Tallin, Estonia. But without the prospect of becoming a foreign service officer, she found the work infuriatingly dull and resigned in May 1939. She was in Paris, considering options, when the war started. She volunteered as an ambulance driver for the French army (private second class), serving at the front until France surrendered in May 1940. Out of a job again, she made her way to London, where she found a clerical position with the military attaché in the American embassy. A short time later, she met Vera Atkins and her life changed forever.

Within the French Section of SOE, Vera Atkins was a bit of a legend. The conservatively dressed, chain-smoking special assistant to the head of "F" Section, Col. Maurice Buckmaster, had no prior experience. In fact, she was not even a British subject. But she had well-placed friends, learned quickly, and was soon helping with recruitment, monitoring agent training, and looking after agent needs while behind the lines in France. F Section supported the resistance in matters of training, logistics, and sabotage. Getting suitable agents to work with the French was a constant problem and Atkins developed a knack for finding good ones.[10] While chatting with Hall at a dinner party and learning of her language skills—French and German, albeit with an American accent—plus her ambulance driving experiences, Atkins sensed she possessed poise under pressure. They met the next day for lunch and Atkins convinced Hall to leave the embassy and join SOE.

Since America was not yet in the war and its citizens could travel freely in unoccupied France, Hall was targeted for duty with cover as a reporter for the *New York Post*. Contrary to some accounts that claim Hall was sent to France without any

---

[9] The brass foot story appeared first in M. R. D. Foot's unclassified official history of SOE (see footnote 1 above) and came from the official classified history of the organization (only declassified in 1998) that he was allowed to read, but not cite, when doing his research in the early 1960s. Pearson's research showed that a solid brass foot would have been too heavy and that rubber was needed for comfort and to minimize noise.

[10] For more detail on Atkins, see Sarah Helm. *A Life In Secrets: The Story of Vera Atkins and the Lost Agents of SOE* (London: Little Brown, 2005).

training,[11] Pearson shows that she completed the standard officer courses, with the exception of the parachute portion. On 23 August 1941, she arrived in Vichy, the capital of unoccupied France, and registered with the embassy. Then she went to Lyon, to begin her work in the field. For the next 14 months, using various aliases—Bridgette LeContre, Marie, Philomène, Germaine—she worked to organize the resistance, help downed fliers escape, provide courier service for other agents, and obtain supplies for the clandestine presses and the forgers—all this while managing to write articles for the *Post* and avoid the Gestapo that had penetrated many of the resistance networks.

In November 1942, when the Allies invaded North Africa and the Nazis occupied all of France, Hall had to flee—she knew too much to risk capture. Her only means of escape was to walk across the Pyrenees through winter snow to Spain, where she was jailed for a few weeks before being allowed to continue to London. Her first request was to return to France. SOE said no, it was too risky, especially with her likeness on a wanted poster. She settled instead for Madrid. But after nearly a year there, she found the duties unbearably boring and requested something more operational. Returning to London in January 1944, she was assigned the unexciting but not unimportant job of briefing agents and officers about to be sent behind the lines in France. She knew that, with the preparations for D-Day underway, the resistance was critically short of radio operators, so she applied and was trained in radio communications—but with no guarantees.

Until then, Hall had paid little attention to a new American organization she had heard about—the Office of Strategic Services (OSS)—that conducted resistance support operations in cooperation with SOE. Now, she made contacts there and decided to transfer if she could be sent back to France to work with the resistance. By March 1944, she was on a motorboat crossing the English Channel headed for the coast of France. Working in disguise as an old woman farmhand, she organized sabotage operations, supported resistance groups as a radio operator and courier, located drop zones for the RAF, and eventually worked with a Jedburgh team to sabotage German military movements. Once again she managed to avoid capture, despite some close calls.

After France was freed, Hall was trained for an OSS assignment in occupied Vienna, where she had once gone to college; however, the war ended before she could get there. When OSS was abolished at the end of September 1945, Hall stayed on in Europe, working for the follow-on organization, eventually named the Central Intelligence Group (CIG). In 1947, she made the transition to the CIA clandestine service. When she reached the mandatory retirement age of 60 in 1966, Virginia Hall left the CIA as a GS-14, never having been allowed to serve in a peacetime station overseas.

The Wolves at the Door does more than chronicle Hall's extraordinary career. Pearson gives vivid detail about Hall driving a crude ambulance loaded with wounded

---

[11] Margret L. Rossiter, *Women in the Resistance* (New York: Praeger, 1986), 191.

while under fire; how she twice escaped the continent; how she got through SOE training with her artificial leg (which she called *Cuthbert*); the agent problems she dealt with, including the discovery of a Gestapo double-agent; her disguises and her cover work as a milkmaid and farmer's helper; and how she arranged the escape of several of her agents from a Gestapo prison. We also see something of this remarkable woman's managerial abilities when Pearson tells how she overcame the reluctance of the French resistance to follow orders from a woman. After the war, Hall's achievements were to be publicly recognized with the presentation of the Distinguished Service Cross by President Harry Truman. She declined the honor, however, preferring to receive the award without publicity from OSS chief Gen. William Donovan, and thus preserve her cover for clandestine work in the postwar era.

In writing this story, Judith Pearson examined the recently released SOE files in the British National Archives and the OSS files in the American National Archives. She interviewed Hall's niece in Baltimore and others who knew and wrote about her, including SOE historian Foot. It is an amazing tale of an unheralded woman intelligence officer way ahead of her time—Virginia Hall was a genuine heroine.

First In: An Insider's Account of How the CIA Spearheaded the War on Terror in Afghanistan

By Gary C. Schroen. New York: Ballantine Books, 2005. 379 pages.

Reviewed by J. Daniel Moore

There have been a number of illuminating accounts of the CIA's involvement in Afghanistan in the period 1980–2001, most of them critical. Such well-regarded studies as the *9/11 Commission Report,* Steve Coll's *Ghost Wars,* Daniel Benjamin and Steve Simon's *The Age of Sacred Terror,* and Ahmed Rashid's *Taliban* detail US missteps in South Asia and foreshadow the terrorist attacks in New York and Washington on September 11, 2001. In contrast, retired CIA officer Gary Schroen's *First In* is a "good news" story for the Agency, recounting the brief, successful, CIA-led operation to assist the Afghan opposition in overthrowing the Islamist Taliban regime in the fall of 2001.

Schroen's memoir is mostly a straightforward account of his role leading the Northern Afghanistan Liaison Team (NALT) from mid-September to the end of October 2001. He opens with the gripping story of the al-Qa'ida-orchestrated murder of legendary ethnic-Tajik commander Ahmed Shah Masood on 9 September 2001 by two Arab assassins posing as journalists. Schroen had met Masood several times during earlier assignments in the region, meetings arranged by Masood's close friend and political aide, Masood Khalili. It is Khalili who is Schroen's chief source for the horrifying account of Masood's assassination through a suicide bombing that almost killed Khalili, as well.

Al-Qa'ida and its Taliban ally surely anticipated that Masood's death would lead to the rapid military collapse of the Tajik-led Northern Alliance, which had been holding out against the stronger Taliban for nearly five years. Instead, the terrorist attacks in the United States two days later sparked the Bush administration's worldwide war against terrorism. The NALT deployed nine days after the 9/11 attacks, joining the Northern Alliance forces north of Kabul. The subsequent CIA-led military operation resulted in the destruction of the Taliban regime by early December, although Usama Bin Ladin and other top al-Qa'ida leaders escaped.

Readers should find of special interest Schroen's account of how the NALT materialized in the days following the attacks. His reaction to the horror of 9/11 is honest and personal. He describes how his colleagues in the Near East Division responded to the televised coverage and details how he received a call at home two days later request-

J. Daniel Moore is a retired CIA operations officer who has field experience in South Asia.

---

ing him to meet the following morning with the chief the Counterterrorist Center, Cofer Black. When Black asked Schroen to take a small team into Afghanistan, link up with the Northern Alliance, and obtain its cooperation to go after Bin Ladin and al-Qa'ida, he accepted without hesitation. He was, after all, highly qualified for the job: He had had three tours in Islamabad working the radical Islamic target, including a last assignment as chief of station; he spoke Farsi; and he already knew many of the senior people in the Northern Alliance.

The speed at which the NALT came together—reaching the Panjshir Valley by 26 September—speaks eloquently of the CIA's flexibility and ability to react in a crisis. Schroen and his deputy assembled the team in short order, with each officer identifying a trusted colleague who brought special skills to the endeavor. Schroen chose a young, talented, Farsi-speaking operations officer with whom he had served in Islamabad. His deputy selected a fellow Special Activities Division officer, a paramilitary expert and former Marine who spoke Russian and wore a corduroy sport coat in meetings with Northern Alliance officials. Three additional specialists joined the team: a former SEAL whose strong organizational skills and high energy got the team kick started and packed up for Afghanistan; a retired Agency officer and Vietnam veteran who served as field medic and more; and a communications genius who kept equipment working in a difficult environment.

The CIA's agility in responding to the 9/11 attacks stood in stark contrast to the difficulties US military special forces encountered in getting "boots on the ground" in Afghanistan. Schroen documents his team's efforts while still in Washington to coordinate planning with special operations officers, who were preoccupied with chains of command and uncertain of their mission and status relative to the CIA. Ultimately, the NALT left for Afghanistan without the special forces representative they had hoped to include. The first special forces team reached the Panjshir Valley on 17 October, nearly a month after the NALT's arrival. More special forces units soon followed, joining other CIA teams already in country. The joint CIA-special forces teams made short work of the Taliban. Agency officers provided the cultural and language expertise, while the military personnel coordinated air and ground fire-support assets. These working relationships remained excellent through the crumbling of Taliban resistance on 6 December.

Schroen played a crucial role in leading the NALT's sometimes painful early negotiations with the Northern Alliance leadership and in interfacing with CIA headquarters. He deftly walked the tightrope between a demanding Tajik-led alliance that sought to promote its own political interests over those of other tribal groups, and a US national security community that seemed to lean too much, in Schroen's view, in the direction of placating Pakistan, once the Taliban's backer and now an advocate of a non-Tajik post-Taliban government. Schroen left the NALT in early November 2001, before the fall of Mazar-e Sharif, Kabul, and Kandahar. His successor, who presided over the final stage of the battle for the capital, appears to have provided the author with colorful details of that phase of the campaign. Leaders of other Agency teams also furnished Schroen with firsthand accounts.

While certain aspects of the Afghan campaign remain classified, *First In* does a good job getting much of the story out to the American public. One marvels at how much detail, some of it politically sensitive, made it into print—so much, in fact, that it raises a disturbing question about whether the publicity might have negative repercussions for the Afghan officials who cooperated with Schroen and the CIA during Operation ENDURING FREEDOM.

First In describes a gung-ho success story for the Bush administration and the CIA. Still, Schroen speaks out in the book's Afterword against what he attests is the administration's relative loss of interest in Afghanistan. With the National Security Council's increasing preoccupation with Iraq after mid-2002, Afghanistan took a back seat in the allocation of financial and personnel resources, he argues, and the possibility of the capture of Bin Ladin and defeat of al-Qa'ida receded.

Schroen is on firm ground when he describes what he personally experienced. When he records events learned second-hand, he relies on anecdotes. When he discusses US policy in the Islamic world, he is merely voicing an opinion. Schroen's foray into the policy realm at the conclusion of *First In* struck this reviewer as a stretch—perhaps the result of a publisher who thought that criticism of the Bush administration by a CIA veteran might sell well. That aside, overall, the action story is an important and compelling one, and Schroen tells it well.

The Castro Obsession

By Don Bohning. Washington, DC: Potomac Books, 2005.

Reviewed by Brian Latell

For almost 50 years, Fidel Castro has relished telling audiences large and small of the hundreds of assassination attempts he has survived. Most recently, in June 2005, he regaled a crowd in a Venezuelan port city, saying it may have been the only time he has traveled abroad when there was no plan afoot to kill him. Such hyperbole has always been an essential ingredient in the imagery of invincibility and cunning that he promotes about himself.

Castro has had no higher priority from the outset of his revolutionary career than his personal security. Once in power he set out immediately to create intelligence and security services, both within and independent of the armed forces controlled by his brother Raul, that have reliably made him one of the world's most physically invulnerable leaders. When traveling abroad he typically surrounds himself with an entourage of hundreds of elite security and support personnel. Cuban intelligence has long been among the best in the world with a demonstrated ability to ferret out potential threats well before they coalesce.

The actual number of assassination attempts against Castro is unknown, but surely many times smaller than the impression he encourages of CIA and Cuban exile rogues perennially plotting against him. Not a single foreign-based assassination plan is known to have come close to succeeding and most, including all of those hatched in the CIA under pressure from the Kennedy administration, were laughably inept.

These are among the main themes that Don Bohning develops in *The Castro Obsession*, an excellent and much needed illumination in a single comprehensive volume of all the strange and counterproductive American covert schemes that Castro has survived. A Latin America reporter and editor for 40 years with the *Miami Herald*, Bohning documents the Kennedy administration's efforts, beginning with the Bay of Pigs and continuing until the assassination in Dallas, to bring Castro down. He is balanced and nuanced, especially when describing some of the zanier ideas that were bandied about at Agency headquarters—an exploding seashell assassination device, a depilatory to root out Castro's signature beard, LSD to cause him to flail into delusional gyrations during a public appearance.

Brian Latell, a former CIA officer and past chairman of the Editorial Board of *Studies in Intelligence*, is a senior associate at the Center for Strategic and International Studies in Washington and author of the recently published book, *After Fidel*. Copyright © 2005 by Brian Latell.

Other authors and congressional investigators—notably the Church Committee in 1976—have covered portions of this ground, but none has tied all the threads together so neatly or made the case with such an abundance of declassified CIA documents and interviews with retired Cuba hands. Bohning quotes several ranking headquarters- and Miami station-based officers who were intimately involved in the 1960s covert campaigns, as well as another who was detailed to the Kennedy White House as a staff coordinator for special operations. Some of them apparently reminisced on the record for the first time.

Bohning's sources were unanimous in their disparagement of Robert Kennedy, and the author clearly sympathizes with them. The attorney general was "obsessed" with Cuba after the Bay of Pigs, a view that White House aide Arthur Schlesinger and other biographers have disputed even while admitting that the anti-Castro Operation MONGOOSE was Bobby Kennedy at his inexplicable worst. It was "his most conspicuous folly," Schlesinger has written. Tom Parrott, the CIA officer detailed to the White House, is quoted scorning the younger Kennedy as "arrogant and overbearing." Bohning adds that Bobby, as the unofficial overseer of Cuba clandestine operations, was "constantly on the phone with anyone and everyone involved, both US officials and Cuban exiles."

The author and his Agency sources are equally critical in describing the air force general whom the Kennedy brothers selected as day-to-day manager of MONGOOSE. Edward Lansdale, who had extensive covert action experience in the Philippines and Vietnam but no knowledge of Cuba, was a "quirky and flamboyant officer" with a chaotic management style. Sam Halpern, a respected senior operations officer who worked on MONGOOSE, told the author that Lansdale was "a con man." Former CIA Director Richard Bissell is quoted from his memoirs commenting that Lansdale's "ideas were impractical" and that he "never had much faith they would be successful." Bissell said: "I was under stern injunction, however, to do everything possible to assist him. The Kennedys wanted action, they wanted it fast."

Former Secretary of State Alexander Haig, who became involved in covert Cuba operations in February 1963 as an aide to the secretary of the army, told the author that Lansdale was "the strangest duck I ever talked to. He was telling me about the Philippines. That's all he wanted to talk about. I didn't get anything on Cuba." Haig said he told his boss, Cyrus Vance, who later also served as secretary of state, that Lansdale was "a dingbat." But Bohning writes that Lansdale nonetheless "moved ahead self-confident and unfazed." He never lost the trust of the Kennedy brothers that he would somehow manage to bring Castro down.

Most in the CIA and the Pentagon had recognized by the middle of 1961, however, that nothing short of American military intervention could achieve that. National intelligence estimates and CIA current analysis had been making the point that Castro's position was rapidly consolidating as pockets of opposition to him were being wiped out. He still enjoyed strong popular support and the Cuban uniformed services had become ruthlessly effective. Previously, many scholars believed that CIA analysts and operations officers were working with profoundly differing sets of assumptions about Castro's staying power after the Bay of Pigs. But Bohning does a good job of showing how skeptical and reluctant most senior operations officers involved in MONGOOSE in fact were as they obediently carried out the administration's designs. Halpern is quoted telling the author that its planning "made no sense at all . . . . It's crazy." Few really thought that the covert operations would have much impact, and certainly not enough to bring down the regime.

Nonetheless, under pressure from the administration, wishful thinking about Castro's vulnerability was indulged. CIA Director John McCone—normally skeptical about the prospects for covert action success in Cuba—told a White House planning meeting that more acute economic hardship on the island would cause the military to oust Fidel. It is not clear if that was his personal opinion, or if analysts had briefed him along those lines, but no such thing was possible then, or at any time since Raul Castro took control of the armed forces in October 1959. Under his leadership, the Cuban military has been the most effective, loyal, and disciplined among all its counterparts in Latin America. Over the four and a half decades of the Castro brothers' political hegemony, there has never been a credible report of coup plotting.

Bohning has done a useful service in bringing together nearly all of the relevant declassified information about covert operations against Castro from 1959 into the second year of Lyndon Johnson's administration. The author cites numerous documents declassified for the Kennedy Assassination Records Review Board and the Church Committee hearings, and other records extracted through Freedom of Information Act requests. He has missed very little in this admirable work.

One interesting bit of missile crisis history that had long baffled scholars, but was finally clarified several years ago with released CIA documents, did not come to Bohning's attention, however. During the run-up to the missile crisis, New York Senator Kenneth Keating was shrill in denouncing the Kennedy administration for minimizing the intensifying Soviet military build-up in Cuba. He insisted on the Senate floor that he had inside information that strategic missiles were being introduced. Bohning did not discover that it was noted playwright, former member of Congress, and ambassador Clare Booth Luce who was Keating's source.

Another, more pivotal, issue that Bohning makes little effort to explain is *why* the Kennedy brothers became so obsessed with Castro and Cuba. In all fairness to the president and the attorney general, it should have been emphasized that the Cuban leader posed a threat of almost incalculable dimensions to John Kennedy's reelection prospects and to critical American interests throughout Latin America and beyond. With the launching of Kennedy's ambitious Alliance for Progress just a month before the Bay of Pigs, his administration went head-to-head with Castro throughout Latin America with competing visions of progressive democratic reform, on the one hand, against violent revolutionary upheaval, on the other.

CIA Director McCone testified before the House Foreign Affairs Committee in February 1963 about Cuban government efforts to promote and support revolution in the region. He said that between 1,000 and 1,500 Latin Americans had traveled to Cuba the year before for ideological and guerrilla warfare training and that more had already gone in early 1963. "In essence," McCone said, "Castro tells revolutionaries from other Latin American countries: 'Come to Cuba: We will pay your way, we will train you in underground organization techniques, in guerrilla warfare, in sabotage and terrorism. We will see to it that you get back to your homeland.'"

Information from Soviet records has recently expanded our knowledge of the enormous scope of Cuban intelligence and subversive activities in Latin America. In the second volume of the *Mitrokhin Archives*, Cambridge professor Christopher Andrew and Vasili Mitrokhin reveal that from 1962 to 1966 a total of 650 Cuban illegals were dispatched through Prague, most of them enroute to Latin America. During those years, powerful guerrilla movements, often employing terrorist methods, became entrenched in several countries.

Bohning might also have emphasized Castro's strategic and military alliance with the Soviet Union as a cause of the Kennedys' obsession. It was not until early December 1961 that Fidel announced he was a Marxist-Leninist, although by then the alliance with Moscow was well advanced. Soviet military supplies were pouring into Cuba during the summer of 1962 just as Operation MONGOOSE was reaching a crescendo. It was not a coincidence. Rather, it may have been inevitable, because of the miscalculations in the White House and the Kremlin, that the superpowers would face off in a nuclear showdown, all because of the Kennedys' Castro obsession.

Don Bohning is not the first author to argue that, through their anti-Castro militance, the Kennedy brothers were responsible for provoking the Cuban missile crisis. Soviet leader Nikita Khrushchev once ruminated about the new Cuban regime to members of his inner circle: "We must not allow the communist infant to be strangled in its crib." Khrushchev went to his grave insisting that he had made the decision to install the missiles in Cuba to defend the revolution against the determined efforts by the Kennedys to overthrow it. Bohning demonstrates with overwhelming evidence the extent to which Castro indeed was in the American crosshairs.

The Intelligence Officer's Bookshelf

Compiled and Reviewed by Hayden B. Peake

This section contains brief reviews of recent books of interest to intelligence professionals and to students of intelligence.

Rob Johnston. ***Analytic Culture in the U.S. Intelligence Community: An Ethnographic Study***. Washington, DC: Central Intelligence Agency, Center for the Study of Intelligence, 2005. 161 pages, footnotes, charts, no index.

Ethnology is the study of cultures by anthropologists. Rob Johnston is an anthropologist who received a Director of Central Intelligence Research Fellowship "to investigate analytic culture, methodology, error and failure within the Intelligence Community using applied anthropological methodology" (xiii). He was also to make recommendations for performance improvement where appropriate. Toward these ends he conducted 489 interviews, observed analysts on the job, and collected data from focus groups. Research began four days after 9/11: This study is the result. While it does not provide a formula for change, it does suggest a path to improvement.

Part one deals with definitions and findings. Many of the areas discussed will be familiar—bias, secrecy, time constraints, incentives, training, and tradecraft. Comments from interviewees are illuminating in their depth and variety. Dr. Johnston's finding on tradecraft as applied to analysis, in particular, may provoke discussion. He sees analysis as a scientific process, not a "practiced skill in a trade or art," a distinction that may influence the rigor of the analytic thought process (17–18).

Part two, the "Ethnography of Analysis," is concerned with the culture of analysis—its terminology, variables, analytic methods, and the concept of the intelligence cycle. That he finds the traditional intelligence cycle inadequate to explain the complex processes involved is not surprising. His alternatives should inspire a lively discussion.

The third part of the study is concerned with "Potential Areas for Improvement." Here he argues that experts predict events no better than Bayesian statistics unless secret data provide an edge. He also points out that most people misuse the term "mirror imaging," and that there is real value in more technologically based instruction for analysts. With regard to prospective employees, he urges that more should be done to acquaint them with the realities of the Intelligence Community and the analysis profession. The final

---

Hayden B. Peake is the curator of the CIA's Historical Intelligence Collection.

---

chapter in this part provides recommendations for a "performance improvement infrastructure" that emphasizes the value of metrics and lessons-learned databases. Here he deals with *what* needs to be done, leaving *how* for another time.

Johnston has examined intelligence analysis from an anthropologist's perspective. The path to professional improvement that he recommends may embrace unfamiliar, even controversial, concepts, but it may also stimulate new approaches while expanding one's vocabulary.

Theodore Shackley and Richard Finney. ***Spymaster: My Life in the CIA.*** Dulles, VA: Potomac Books, Inc., 2005. 309 pages, endnotes, photos, index.

This book is surprising both for what it says and what it does not say, as well as for the style used to say it. Moreover, it is not quite a memoir or a biography. Shackley never tells how he came to join the CIA. For that and other background data one must read the excellent foreword by former CIA officer Hugh Tovar and the preface by Shackley's coauthor and former CIA colleague, Richard Finney. What Shackley does do is comment selectively on various aspects of his career, including some principal assignments and his controversial but effective management style. He also includes small professional gems about the value of open source background reading before beginning a new assignment.

The non-traditional format of the book becomes apparent in chapter one, "Espionage," which begins with a statement on the importance of HUMINT. Then, on page two, Shackley arrives in Nürmberg, Germany, to begin his first overseas assignment in 1953. He then tells how he learned the basics of agent recruiting and handling while providing some examples. In chapter two, "Counterintelligence," he discusses the four counterintelligence principles he deems important and then illustrates them with firsthand comments on agent and defector cases familiar to many—from Michael Goleniewski, who exposed the KGB mole in MI6 (George Blake), to Kim Philby and Aldrich Ames. For reasons not clear, he includes a separate, though interesting, chapter on other defector cases later in the book. His comments on counterintelligence end with a fair appraisal of the CIA's long-time chief of counterintelligence, James Angleton.

The third chapter, "Knavish Tricks," covers covert action, which he says at the outset "always held a special fascination for me" (38). Here he discusses what covert action is and gives some historical examples of how it has been part of American intelligence since the revolutionary war. Then he shows that it was also a major part of KGB and CIA operations during the Cold War, although not always working flawlessly.

The balance of the book concentrates on some of Shackley's principal assignments, while omitting others without comment. First, there is his role in Miami as Chief of Operations under his mentor, Bill Harvey, who headed Task

Force W, established at the direction of Attorney General Robert Kennedy to achieve regime change in Cuba. Shackley points out that agents handled by this station were the first to locate and identify the Soviet missiles in Cuba, subsequently photographed by a U-2 in October 1962.

After a brief return to Berlin, Shackley was assigned to Laos and then to Vietnam, and he deals with these tours in considerable detail. He was clearly most pleased with his service in Laos, but it was in Vietnam that he endured the controversy surrounding the death of a Vietnamese suspected by the Army Special Forces of being a double agent. Charges that the CIA condoned the killing have been consistently denied. Shackley explains the circumstances, and his explanation correlates well with other studies of the case.[1]

In the final chapter, Shackley offers his thoughts on intelligence community reform ranging from greater use of non-official cover and a single congressional oversight committee to a director of national intelligence, a position he first advocated in 1992. For those who expected a more expansive tale of clandestine operations, *Spymaster* may be something of a disappointment. On the other hand, what Shackley was able to give is extremely valuable—a first-hand account by someone involved in operations at a critical juncture, with lessons for all.

Richard Posner. ***Preventing Surprise Attacks: Intelligence Reform in the Wake of 9/11.*** Lanham, MD: Bowman & Littlefield Publishers, Inc., 2005. 218 pages, footnotes, index.

The editor of the *New York Times Book Review* asked US Court of Appeals (Chicago) Judge Richard Posner to review the 9/11 Commission Report.[2] Judge Posner found the report, despite some flaws, to be "a lucid, even riveting, narrative of the attacks, the events leading up to them, and the immediate response to them . . . an improbable literary triumph."[3] When author Peter Berkowitz[4] suggested he expand the review into a book, he accepted the challenge.

The result is an articulate assessment of the 9/11 Report recommendations and the consequent rapid congressional and White House response manifest in the *Intelligence Reform Act of 2004*.[5] At the outset, he finds some aspects of the report troubling. For example, he suggests that investigative findings should have been sufficient, with recommendations left to the professionals. He sees

---

[1] See, for example, David Corn, *Blond Ghost: Ted Shackley and the CIA's Crusades* (New York: Simon and Schuster, 1994), 195ff.

[2] 9/11 *Commission Report: Final Report of the National Commission on Terrorist Attacks upon the United States* (New York: Barnes and Noble, 2004).

[3] Richard Posner, "The 9/11 Report: A Dissent," *New York Times Book Review*, 29 August 2004: 1.

[4] Peter Berkowitz, *Terrorism, the Laws of War, and the Constitution: Debating the Enemy Combatant Cases* (Stanford, CA: Hoover Institution Press, 2005).

[5] *Intelligence Reform and Terrorism Prevention Act of 2004,* Title VI, § 6001 (a).

this as "the same mistake as combining intelligence and policy" (6). Similarly, he is concerned that the insistence on report unanimity "deprives the decisionmakers of a full range of alternatives" and leads to "second choice alternatives" (7). Finally, he suggests that the participation of relatives of the 9/11 victims was an unnecessary distraction.

But the central issues of the book have to do with the history of surprise attacks, and the kind of intelligence needed to meet that and other threats. The chapter on surprise provides a thoughtful background for the chapters on the principles and organization of intelligence. His conclusion is straightforward: "Surprise attacks cannot reliably be prevented" (97). "The best one can hope for," he suggests, "is that an intelligence service be able to anticipate most surprise attacks . . . with fewest false alarms" (107).

In his chapter on principles of organization, the judge makes clear that "reorganization is a questionable response to a problem that is not a problem of organization." When the consumers and producers of intelligence are not clamoring for reorganization," Posner concludes, "those on the outside should not impose it." Although he favors separating the counterintelligence mission from the FBI, he is a realist and recognizes that this is unlikely to happen.

Beyond the thoughtful analysis and practical suggestions, it is worth noting that *Preventing Surprise Attacks* makes a fine text for a course on national intelligence. It covers the basic topics, is thoroughly documented with open sources—several from CIA authors and *Studies in Intelligence* articles—and is short enough to please any student. A very valuable addition to the literature.

Jayna Davis. ***The Third Terrorist: The Middle East Connection to the Oklahoma City Bombing***. Nashville, TN: WND Books, 2004. 355 pages, endnotes, index.

In his analysis of the events leading to 9/11, author Peter Lance includes a chapter on the Oklahoma City bombing of the Alfred P. Murrah Federal Building on 19 April 1995.[6] Although his investigation was not complete, he did find that witness statements suggesting "a Mideast connection to the blast . . . [were] circumstantial but worthy of review." Jayna Davis's *The Third Terrorist* provides that review. Former Director of Central Intelligence R. James Woolsey's dust jacket comment notes that " . . . Jayna Davis's near-decade of brave, thorough, and dogged investigative reporting effectively shifts the burden of proof to those who would still contend that McVeigh and Nichols executed the 1995 Oklahoma City bombing without the support of a group or groups from the Middle East."

---

[6] Peter Lance, *1000 Years For Revenge: International Terrorism and the FBI—The Untold Story* (New York: HarperCollins, 2003), 308ff.

Davis's story concentrates on one additional participant—called John Doe #2 by the FBI and whom she identifies—who was seen by several witnesses with McVeigh prior to and on the day of the bombing. But her investigation also identified 11 other suspects with varying degrees of involvement. Evidence for their participation comes from 38 sworn affidavits from witnesses who, with a few exceptions, did not know each other. Davis convinced a former FBI special agent; State Department, CIA, and DIA counterterrorism analysts; and TV and newspaper journalists—including from the *Wall Street Journal,* which conducted its own investigation[7]—that her evidence was solid and worthy of a response from the government. But all that her persistence achieved was the loss of her job as an investigative reporter for the Oklahoma City NBC-TV station.

The Third Terrorist takes the reader through the author's painstaking collection of evidence that is dismissed by the federal authorities. It is well written, thoroughly documented, and a good example of research in open sources.

Nigel West, ed. ***The Guy Liddell Diaries—1939–1945: MI5's Director of Counter-Espionage in World War II***, Vols. I & II. London: Routledge, 2005. 629 pages, appendix, glossary, index.

In the movie *Five Fingers*, James Mason played a Nazi spy codenamed "Cicero," who, as the valet of the British ambassador in Turkey, photographed secret Foreign Office documents during World War II. The film was an early example of Oliver Stone history: Little beyond the spy's name was factual. Cicero's memoirs told his side of the story, including his successful escape, but he did not know how MI5 became suspicious of him.[8] *The Guy Liddell Diaries* fill that gap and many others.

Without telling anyone besides his trusted secretary, Margo Huggins, Guy Liddell dictated his thoughts on the day's events from August 1939 to June 1945. The resulting 12 volumes were declassified in 2002. The entries reveal wartime counterintelligence operations, the MI5 turf battles with MI6 and SOE, the conflicts between J. Edgar Hoover and the MI6 station in New York headed by William Stephenson, and some surprises. In the latter category, we learn that Cicero was not the only penetration of the embassy in Ankara. There were two others: One was the ambassador's chauffeur; the other was never identified. On the home front, many entries describe the intricacies of the double-cross system and its use of the ULTRA signals intercept material from Bletchley Park to monitor the effectiveness of the deceptions. Not all went smoothly for Liddell—there were three internal inquiries into possible MI5 penetrations. But he survived, although one mole, Liddell's assistant, Anthony Blunt, was not suspected and only exposed as a Soviet agent in 1964. Besides

---

[7] Micah Morrison, "The Iraq Connection," *Wall Street Journal,* 5 September 2002.
[8] Elyesa Bazna, *I Was Cicero* (New York: Harper and Row, 1962). Bazna, an Albanian, was Cicero's true name.

Blunt, the familiar names Kim Philby and Guy Burgess are mentioned from time to time, but there is not a hint that Liddell suspected that they, too, were Soviet agents.

To set the stage, editor Nigel West has added an introduction with biographic details of the cello-playing Liddell. He has also included clarifying comments regarding names and acronyms. For reasons of space, some of the administrative diary entries are excluded.[9] Nevertheless, the result is a unique slice of counterintelligence history valuable to historian, student, and espionage aficionado alike.

Richard C. S. Trahair. ***Encyclopedia of Cold War Espionage, Spies, and Secret Operations***. Westwood, CT: Greenwood Press, 2004. 472 pages, bibliographic essay, glossary, chronology, index.

At least seven dictionaries and encyclopedias of intelligence have been published since 2000.[10] While their quality varies, the current offering is a strong competitor for a position near the bottom of any ranking. Many of the errors involve dates: for example, James Angleton was not head of counterintelligence at the CIA from 1951 to 1973 (9); his tenure was from 1954–1974. Cambridge spy Anthony Blunt did not confess in 1963; it was 1964 (21). The British Secret Intelligence Service (SIS/MI6) was formed in 1909, not 1946 (415). OSS was disbanded in September not December 1945 (51). And Vitaly Yurchenko defected in August not September 1985 (345).

Other entries combine errors of facts and dates, as for example the description of the Elizabeth Bentley case. Trahair writes that she went to the FBI in August 1945 and agreed to become a double agent within the Communist Party of the United States of America (16–17). She did neither. She went to the FBI in November 1945 and made a detailed statement after which she briefly and unsuccessfully worked against the NKVD. Furthermore, the statement that Bentley's "efforts initiated the case against Alger Hiss" is incorrect; that honor goes to Whittaker Chambers.

Then comes the category of plain factual error: George Blake was not "a double agent employed by the British secret service SIS," nor was he in the SOE (25); he was just a KGB penetration agent or mole. Other examples abound: Whittaker Chambers never went to Moscow (46); Donald Maclean was not assigned to work on the "development of the atom bomb" (180); Cambridge spy

---

[9] The British National Archives Web site provides access to every entry for a per-page fee.

[10] Norman Polar and Thomas Allen, *SPY BOOK* (New York: Random House, 2004); Rodney Carlisle, ed., *The Encyclopedia of Intelligence and Counterintelligence* (Armonk, NY: M. E. Sharpe, 2005); Allan Swenson and Michael Benson, *The Complete Idiot's Guide to the CIA* (Indianapolis, IN: Alpha Books, 2003); Richard Bennett. *Espionage: The Encyclopedia of Spies and Secrets* (London: Virgin Books, 2002); Denis Collins, *SPYING: The Secret History of History* (New York: Black Dog & Leventhal Publishers, Inc., 2004); John Simeone and David Jacobs, *The Complete Idiot's Guide to the FBI* (Indianapolis, IN: Alpha Books, 2003)—all of which have been reviewed by *Studies in Intelligence*.

Kim Philby was not a member of the Communist Party of Great Britain; Anthony Blunt was not "the first of the KGB's Magnificent Five"(264), he was the fourth agent recruited; and William Casey was never "OSS station chief in London" (45). Another completely erroneous and confusing comment on the OSS states that it was "the temporary organization of eight intelligence agencies under the direction of William J. Donovan . . . renamed OSS" in April 1942 (65). In a similar vein it is hard to explain why Trahair thought former NSA employee Ronald Pelton ever worked for the Canadian Security Service (346). A final example in this category is the statement in the chronology that "MI5 leaked the secret Zinoviev letter." Foreign office chief historian Gill Bennett shows in her study of the affair that it was a conscious decision of the government through SIS/MI6.[11]

In several cases, Trahair defies his own sources. One example will suffice: Soviet agent Judith Coplon was not, as alleged, an "employee of the Federal Bureau of Investigation (FBI)" (53). She worked for the Justice Department, as is made abundantly clear in the definitive book on the case, *The Spy Who Seduced America*, which is cited as one of his sources.[12] Lastly, the glossary entries deserve a health warning. There is no such thing as a "defector-in-place"; the term is an oxymoron. The term "double agents" is used inaccurately: Of the 28 "double agents" listed on page xiv, 22 are incorrect. The curious glossary entry for Arnold Deutsch says he recruited his own NKVD bosses, Alexander Orlov and Theodore Maly, and was "running the Woolwich Arsenal spy ring"—all untrue.

Only a few of the many errors and discrepancies are mentioned here. All could have been avoided with the exercise of due diligence. But that burden should not be placed on the reader, especially a student. *Caveat Emptor*.

Al J. Venter. ***Iran's Nuclear Option: Tehran's Quest for the Atom Bomb***. Philadelphia, PA: Casement, 2005. 451 pages, endnotes, appendix, photos, index.

In October 2003, Iran acknowledged that it was indeed producing weapons-grade uranium as part of a two-decades-long clandestine nuclear program. Journalist Al Venter is convinced that the Islamic republic is on a march toward the acquisition of nuclear weapons and makes a strong case in *Iran's Nuclear Option*. A native of South Africa, he witnessed that country's development of an atomic bomb, and he devotes a chapter to the parallels that emerge.

---

[11] Gill Bennett, *History Notes: "A most extraordinary and mysterious business": The Zinoviev Letter of 1924* (London: Foreign & Commonwealth Office, General Services Command, 1999), 40.
[12] Marcia and Thomas Mitchell, *The Spy Who Seduced America: Lies and Betrayal in the Heart of the Cold War—The Judith Coplon Story* (Montpelier, VT: Invisible Cities Press, 2002)—reviewed in *Studies in Intelligence* 47, no. 2 (2002).

After brief consideration of the history of the republic and the consequences of the Islamic revolution in 1979, Venter looks in substantial detail at how close the Iranians are to building the bomb—he concludes nobody really knows—and who is helping and has helped them. On this last point, he argues that "at the heart of Iran's ongoing nuclear programs stands Russia," though there are also links to Pakistan and North Korea. He quotes sources who worked at the International Atomic Energy Agency who are very critical of the "weak-kneed" approach taken by the agency to its inspection responsibilities. The idea that Iran's nuclear program is "designed to meet only the country's energy needs and has absolutely no military use" is dismissed on considerable evidence, not the least of which is Iran's almost "unlimited supplies of oil" (125).

Perhaps the most disturbing element of Venter's analysis is the discussion of the alternatives available to the West should Iran declare or demonstrate nuclear capability and belligerent intent. What could and would Israel do? Iran is much farther from Israel than Iraq and the Iranian nuclear facilities are well dispersed. Moreover the location of all its facilities may not be known. Then there is the question of Iran's relationship to al-Qa'ida and other terrorist groups and rogue states—would they be permitted access to bombs under certain conditions? The intelligence required to prevent these acts, he suggests, will be almost impossible to acquire in light of the near inability to penetrate terrorist secrecy. Diplomatic efforts to deflect Iran's nuclear ambitions do not seem promising either, although the author sees some hope in the Libyan precedent. Venter cannot be faulted for glossing over an alarming, even frightening, situation. *Iran's Nuclear Option* is well documented and makes clear that the failure of the West's anti-proliferation program will also produce options, all unpleasant.

Paul Sperry. ***Infiltration: How Muslim Spies and Subversives Have Penetrated Washington***. Nashville, TN: Nelson Current, 2005. 359 pages, endnotes, index.

The 9/11 Commission report reached the conclusion that "Our enemy is twofold: al-Qa'ida, a stateless network of terrorists that struck us on 9/11; and a radical ideological movement in the Islamic world . . . which has spawned terrorist groups and violence across the globe" (xxiv). *Infiltration* looks at what these groups plan to do and how they intend to do it.

Author Paul Sperry lets the Islamist radicals answer the first question. According to Abdurahman M. Alamondi, founder of the American Muslim Council, "the goal of Muslims in America is to turn the U.S. into an Islamic State, even if it takes a hundred years" (xi). One-time University of South Florida professor Sami Al-Arian adds that "What is needed is the dismantling of the cultural system of the West . . . . Our presence in North America gives us a unique opportunity to monitor, explore and follow up. We should be able to infiltrate the sensitive intelligence agencies or the embassies to collect information" (xxiii).

From the 1930s on, the communists in America had similar goals. They tried to achieve them through subversion of the government. The Islamists, suggests Sperry, will try that, too, but they have one big advantage—radical religion. While recognizing the unyielding devotion of its followers, *Infiltration* does not argue the spiritual aspects of Islam. First, it shows how the religion influences the Islamists, as opposed to the non-radical adherents. Then the author focuses on the principal advantage of functioning within a religion in the United States—tax exempt terrorism. The chapters on the terror support network will be of special interest to intelligence community readers, particularly those portions describing the financial and educational enterprises along Route 7 in Virginia.

Sperry tackles some politically sensitive topics such as the practical side of racial profiling, the conflict over human rights and security, the fifth column of terrorists in various government organizations, and the current state of the Homeland Security Department. Sprinkled throughout the book are stories that illustrate how difficult it is to deal with the Islamists who know US law well. In the final chapter, Sperry provides two lists: One gives the reasons why the "death-loving jihadists" are "the perfect enemy" (312); the second gives 10 ways to defeat "the perfect enemy," but no guarantees. Sperry sees the United States "hacking at the branches of terrorism rather than striking at the roots" (328). In short, *Infiltration* identifies the problems well and is worth serious attention for that reason alone. It leaves to the analysts and decisionmakers the determination as to the best solutions.

Katherine A. S. Sibley. ***Red Spies in America: Stolen Secrets and the Dawn of the Cold War***. Lawrence: University Press of Kansas, 2004. 370 pages, endnotes, bibliography, photos, index.

Katherine Sibley holds the history chair at St. Joseph's University in Philadelphia. Her book is about domestic counterintelligence in America from the 1930s to the present. Three points are worth noting at the outset. First, it is well documented, including FBI and Soviet material only recently released. Second, it is well written. Third, all of the cases have been written about in other books, but Sibley looks at them from a new perspective.

To provide background, Sibley begins with a survey of Soviet espionage from the end of World War I to the late 1930s. She concludes with a chapter on Soviet spying in America since World War II. The four chapters in between deal with Soviet espionage in the period from the late 1930s to the end of the war. Most other books that study US counterintelligence during this same period focus on the Cold War aspects of the cases since that is when they came to public attention and, in certain instances, to trial. This approach has left an impression that FBI counterintelligence did not really attack the Soviet espionage threat until after World War II. The reality, as Sibley sees it, is otherwise. In her words, the FBI "recognized the growing infiltration of Soviet spies *before* the Cold War and made limited, but nevertheless pioneering efforts to stop them."

To substantiate this position, she reviews selected prewar and wartime cases of military industrial espionage, the initial indications of atomic espionage, the role of the American communist party, the congressional involvement, the political circumstances that contributed to the Soviet successes, and how the FBI dealt with the unanticipated threat during wartime. A key issue is how the cases came to the attention of the Bureau. She explains that some leads came from informants in the communist party and surveillance of its members. Other cases grew out of investigations into the personnel of the Soviet purchasing organization in America (AMTORG), based on leads from a foreign intelligence service. Still others developed after a disgruntled NKGB officer sent Director J. Edgar Hoover an anonymous letter identifying the personnel in the New York and Washington residencies. Where cases could have been handled better—for example, the failure to act on Walter Krivitsky's and Whittaker Chambers's attempts to expose Soviet espionage prior to the war— she says so candidly. But a key aspect of the FBI counterintelligence program is omitted: The FBI was in a reactive mode. As *Red Spies In America* perhaps unintentionally shows, when espionage cases did turn up, little was done until after the war. In short, the Soviet espionage networks worked without major disruption during the war and were only shut down after it ended. Professor Sibley's thesis is not proved.

Alexander Kouzminov. ***Biological Espionage: Special Operations of the Soviet and Russian Foreign Intelligence Services in the West***. Mechanicsburg, PA: Stackpole Books, 2005. 192 pages, bibliography, appendix, glossary, index.

In 1982, the Biological Faculty of Moscow State University selected Alexander Kouzminov for doctoral study. Even before he received his Ph.D., he joined the KGB's foreign intelligence service. In 1992, after a promising and exciting 10 years, he resigned when KGB corruption continued after the end of the Soviet Union. After two years of civilian life in Russia, he and he wife emigrated to the West.

Kouzminov decided to write this book because he is concerned that Russia is pursuing a biological warfare capability and perhaps even testing agents on unsuspecting nations. He speculates that in addition to the SARS epidemic that began in Hong Kong, the "inexplicable infections that affected wild and domestic stock as well as humans in China . . . in 1997, foot and mouth disease in England in 2001, two plague epidemics in Western India in September and October 1994 . . . are likely results of secret biological research experiments or accidental releases of new anti-crop and anti-livestock weapons into the open environment" (150). Despite international agreements to terminate such programs, he is convinced that they continue in Russia and the West and are a danger to the world. Unfortunately, he offers no documentation, a major weakness of the book.

Biological Espionage provides a detailed description of Directorate S—the KGB action element for these programs—and the tradecraft associated with the recruiting, training, and handling of illegals. He also describes how the KGB/SVR places illegals in businesses in the principal Western countries and what they are trained to do. And although he suggests the program is still very active and useful, the cases mentioned lack specifics and documentation.

True names do appear from time to time as in the case of Vitali Yurchenko, who defected to the CIA in Rome in August 1985 only to redefect on 2 November of the same year. Kouzminov states flatly that Yurchenko was given psychotropic drugs after his "successful 'action-movie-escape' from the CIA's control" to make sure he had not been "recruited as a double agent." Then comes a shocker: Kouzminov declares that Yurchenko was given the Order of the Red Star for his successful CIA "infiltration operation" (107). The reader is left to ponder the inconsistency.

Kouzminov is sincere in his warnings about the dangers of biological warfare. As to what should be done, he offers little more than hope that the "world community of scientists" will cooperate and prevent bio-warfare from becoming a weapon of international terrorism. His arguments should not be dismissed out of hand, but without documentation of any kind they cannot be accepted as fact.

David Christopher Arnold. *Spying From Space: Constructing America's Satellite Command and Control Systems*. College Station: Texas A&M University Press, 2005. 209 pages, endnotes, bibliography, photos, index.

"Once it goes up, who cares where it comes down?" said the lyrics of Tom Lehrer's Harvard drinking song about rocket scientist Werner von Braun. David Arnold answers that question in this book on satellites in space. From the first successful Corona flight in 1961 to the present, the Air Force Satellite Control Facility (AFSCF) and its successor organizations have communicated with satellites, giving them instructions, keeping track of their orbital conditions, and helping to make sure they land on target.

As told by David Arnold for the first time, AFSCF started by addressing common sense questions about making satellites do what is needed once in orbit. The solutions required totally new techniques and technology, contractors, and organizations. Using the rapid developments in satellite systems in the 1960s as his baseline, Arnold describes the systems' evolution, the contractors involved, and the ground-tracking-stations' hardware, location problems, and routine operation.

Interspersed with the technical and hardware issues, Arnold devotes considerable attention to the persistent turf battles that occurred among internal air force elements as well as various national level organizations. Some involved competition for a larger part of the space mission and, thus, budget. Others involved the Air Force's preference for an all blue suit operation when the links to the National Reconnaissance Office and the CIA made that impractical. Arnold deals with these and other stories, revealing details that influence day-to-day operations that are seldom discussed.

Without the ability to control satellites in space, the National Reconnaissance Program could not have succeeded. The AFSCF met that need, and David Arnold's story of how they did it is well documented and well told.

Michael Turner. **Why Secret Intelligence Fails**. Dulles, VA: Potomac Books, Inc., 2005. 217 pages, endnotes, bibliography, glossary, index.

Michael Turner, a former CIA analyst and now professor of international affairs at Alliant International University, San Diego, has written an intelligence primer that is very nearly up to date. It ends just before the post of Director of National Intelligence was filled. He wrote the book because, as an analyst, he could "discern little difference between what made for success and what sparked failure." He does not indicate whether he resolved the dilemma (xiii). His thesis is "that the roots of intelligence failures are embedded in the intelligence cycle and can only be addressed by measures that confront specific dysfunctions in the intelligence process" (13). The book is devoted to validation of this point by discussing the organizational players; reviewing the traditional intelligence cycle and the bureaucratic linkages involved in its functioning; and pondering some analytic techniques—for example, "total information awareness" (TIA) and Doug MacEachin's "linchpin" approach. In chapter three, "Pitfalls of American Intelligence," Turner sets out the "historical forces and structural imperatives [that] together have created a uniquely American 'intelligence ethos . . . .'" By way of clarification, he adds that this refers to "a series of cultural principles"—each of which he discusses—that are specific to "the highly secretive and shadowy world of intelligence." The "deleterious aspects of the eight principles combine with bureaucratic pathologies to account for the majority of intelligence failures. Structural pathologies permeate the entire intelligence process, making them the most significant barriers to successful intelligence" (50). While this chapter lacks a degree of intuitive lucidity, others discuss issues—separation of intelligence from law enforcement, the approaches taken by foreign intelligence services, collection, and dissemination—with less mind-numbing elegance.

On the point of what caused some of the intelligence failures mentioned, he is careful not to argue that corrections will come *only* with organizational change. He argues that "the human element has as much to do with failures of secret intelligence as do structural factors." But then he muddies the issue by suggesting that "taking human failings into account does little good, however, for an intelligence process that intrinsically contains the seeds of failure" (145). Why this should be so, and what to do about it if it is, is not made clear.

In the end, the reader is left with a good summary of the elements of the intelligence profession and a number of issues that should stimulate thinking. But we never do learn just why secret intelligence fails.

Gary Kern, ed. ***Walter G. Krivitsky: MI5 Debriefing & Other Documents on Soviet Intelligence***. Riverside, CA: Xenos Books, 2004. 229 pages, bibliography, glossary, index.

In 1939, Walter Krivitsky, one of the first GRU defectors to the United States, wrote a book on Soviet espionage and testified before Congress on the subject. In both cases, he named some Soviet agents and indicated he knew others in America. The State Department debriefed him on passport matters, but the FBI declined to investigate his counterintelligence claims. Had they done so, Alger Hiss, the atom spies, the Cambridge Five, and many other moles in our government, all of whom were neutralized after the war—would have been identified. Krivitsky made the same offer to the British, and they had him sent over in early 1940. He gave them more than 100 agents, at least two of whom were code clerks. Before he could testify again before Congress, Krivitsky was found shot dead in the Bellevue Hotel (now, The George) near Union Station, Washington, DC.

The British waited more than 60 years to declassify the report of Krivitsky's debriefing, done by MI5 officer, Jane Archer. Author Gary Kern obtained a copy of the Krivitsky debriefing and has reproduced it in this book together with his congressional testimony and some material related to Krivitsky's stay in France after his initial defection.[13] The MI5 debriefing contains the sketchy references to the Philby and Maclean (some say Cairncross) so often mentioned in the literature. There are also specific references to NKVD Gen. Alexander Orlov, already in the United States. Neither MI5 nor the FBI followed up. The case of Orlov is particularly maddening since he had helped recruit Philby (and handled him in Spain), Burgess, and Maclean. Furthermore, several of the KGB agents who would become atom spies in America had worked for Orlov. Yet he remained in hiding until 1953. Besides the MI5 debriefing, Kern has included Krivitsky's views on analysis, and his testimony before Congress.

These are primary source documents. One can learn from them how an interrogation is conducted, what items should be covered, and how they should be reported. They should be of great interest and real value to students, counterintelligence analysts, and all those who continue to marvel at the early days of counterintelligence in America.

---

[13] Gary Kern, *A Death In Washington: Walter G. Krivitsky and the Stalinist Terror* (New York: Enigma Books, 2004). This is the most complete and well-written case study on a Soviet defector ever to be published in English. If reading only one counterintelligence case study, this is the one to chose.

Mikel Dunham. *Buddha's Warriors: The Story of the CIA-Backed Tibetan Freedom Fighters, the Chinese Invasion, and the Ultimate Fall of Tibet*. New York: Penguin, 2004. 434 pages, footnotes, bibliography, index.

In 1970, John MacGregor, better known to some at the time as CIA officer John Waller, published a book on the early history of Tibet.[14] In 1997, retired CIA officer Roger E. McCarthy published his book,[15] which describes his role in support of the CIA's assistance to the Tibetan resistance to China's occupation of Tibet, which began in 1950. Now author-artist Mikel Dunham has told another side of the Tibetan resistance story, for the first time from the point of view of the Tibetan participants.

The Chinese occupation of Tibet was gradual. By 1957, the CIA was training and supplying the resistance. But the Chinese kept increasing the number of their troops and in 1959 the Dalai Lama was forced to flee. The CIA program came to an end when Nixon and Mao agreed to establish diplomatic relations in the early 1970s. China made cessation of the Tibetan support a condition of recognition (382). Today, there are more Chinese in Tibet than Tibetans (6).

The story of what happened in between is well told by Dunham. The resistance fighters he interviewed recall their reaction to the American training and assistance program. They also address, if not explain, how they could take up arms when their religion, Buddhism, the ultimate advocate of nonviolence, prohibits such behavior. The impetus, in part, was practical: "How could the Dalai Lama be protected if we had no weapons . . . ?" (191). The warriors the CIA trained were parachuted back into Tibet to help the resistance on the ground. The American weapons and supplies were much needed, but fighting tactics remained Tibetan, including the custom of never taking prisoners (219). As a consequence of possible Chinese retaliation, they all agreed to accept poison capsules that could be used in the event of capture. Even after 1970, a resistance element operated out of a base in Nepal near the Tibetan border until the Nepalese government was pressured by the Chinese into closing it down, too.

The CIA pullout was disheartening to Americans and Tibetans alike—they did not think a diplomatic solution was possible. Despite the diplomatic complications created by dealing with the various nations involved with the Dalai Lama's fate—India, China, Nepal, Bangladesh, and the United States—the politicians had won the day. Dunham ends the book with his interview of the Dalai Lama. When asked why he thought America agreed to help, the Dalai Lama replied: "I do not think that they came to help out of genuine sympathy or genuine concern . . . ." But when it came to individuals, he added, "they developed some kind of genuine feeling. That I appreciate."

---

[14] John MacGregor. *TIBET: A Chronicle of Exploration* (London: Routledge & Kegan Paul, 1970).
[15] Roger E. McCarthy. *Tears of the Lotus: Accounts of Tibetan Resistance to the Chinese Invasion, 1950–1962* (Jefferson, NC: McFarland & Company, Inc., Publishers, 1997).

Buddha's Warriers is a valuable work for several reasons. First, it makes clear how difficult opposing China can be, on both military and political fronts. Second, it demonstrates that an inadequately supported covert action cannot succeed. Third, it provides a seldom seen example of the human side of the covert action operation in Tibet. Finally, it shows the dedication and bravery of the CIA officers who worked long and hard to accomplish a difficult mission under perilous circumstances.

Jennet Conant. *109 East Palace: Robert Oppenheimer and the Secret City of Los Alamos.* New York: Simon and Schuster, 2005. 424 pages, note on sources, photos, index.

New employees were told only to report to 109 East Palace Avenue, Santa Fe, New Mexico. There they received their security badge and transportation to the Los Alamos laboratories some 60 miles away, where they would work on the Manhattan Project. The story of the building of the atomic bomb has been told before, both from a technical and bureaucratic perspective. Jennet Conant tells the same story, in non-technical terms, but her focus is on life in the "secret city" as it was then—the leaky faucets, the need for barbers, the ever present security hassles, and, especially, the often prickly personal relationships between wives and scientists and the military.[16]

Los Alamos was built on a mountain top "to keep . . . information from getting out" (101). The Army was responsible for physical security; the FBI, for personnel security. That both failed came as a postwar shock, especially to those who thought so highly of Klaus Fuchs as a babysitter.[17] Conant provides a new look at how army intelligence and the FBI attempted to prevent breaches. No one was exempt from scrutiny. *New York Times* reporter, William L. Laurence, the only journalist to visit the site, required a personal letter from Maj. Gen. Leslie Groves, the Manhattan Project director. At one point, military intelligence Capt. Peer de Silva, who would later find a rewarding career in the CIA, reported that "J. R. Oppenheimer is playing a key part in the attempt of the Soviet Union to secure, by espionage, highly secret information which is vital to the United States." Gen. Groves was concerned, but decided Oppenheimer was "absolutely essential to the project." To ease reservations over Oppenheimer's loyalty, Groves appointed de Silva head of security at Los Alamos.

109 East Palace is based on interviews and papers from former workers. Conant shows how in times of adversity and austere living conditions, much can be accomplished.

---

[16] Jennet Conant is the granddaughter of James B. Conant, director of the National Defense Research Committee and deputy director of the Office of Scientific Research and Development during World War II. He worked closely with Oppenheimer.

[17] For reasons not explained, Harvard graduate and Soviet agent Ted Hall, who was at least as damaging as Fuchs, is not mentioned.

Kenneth M. Pollack. ***The Persian Puzzle: The Conflict Between Iran and America.*** New York: Random House, 2004. 529 pages, endnotes, bibliography, maps, index.

Nineteenth century Britain concluded that "Persia . . . was destined by her geographical situation to play a part in the future history of the East altogether disproportionate to her size . . . ."[18] In *The Persian Puzzle,* former CIA analyst Ken Pollack shows that Persia—today's Iran—has exceeded this prediction and become not only a major factor in the world political balance, but the nemesis of the United States as well.

To comprehend why this is so, Pollack argues that one must understand the history and perspective of both countries before trying to formulate solutions to current problems. Toward this end, he reviews the 7,000-year history of the Persian empire and the major events that shaped the nation that became Iran. For Iranians, he suggests that the critical determinant of the country's relationship with America was the 1953 coup that overthrew the Mossadegh government and restored the Shah to power. That this event plays such an important role may come as a surprise to those who lived through it—Americans are "serial amnesiacs," Pollack suggests (xxi). For Americans, on the other hand, the defining image of Iran is the hostage crisis of 1979–81. *The Persian Puzzle* examines the impact of these differing perceptions on the relationship of the two countries for each administration since 1980. The book stresses that all attempts to improve relations since the hostage crisis have failed. Nevertheless, with Iran in the terror business and pushing on the nuclear weapons door, solutions must be found—war is not recommended.

In his final chapter, Dr. Pollack completes the Persian puzzle as he has defined it, only to suggest that having the finished picture does not provide a solution to the problems it depicts. It does, however, clarify them to some extent and he offers a series of policy options to that end. *The Persian Puzzle* makes clear how Iran's political, religious, and military history influences how it thinks and acts the way it does. It then leaves to our leaders the task of resolving differences in an atmosphere shaped by historical rage.

Rose Mary Sheldon. ***Intelligence Activities in Ancient Rome: Trust in the Gods, but Verify.*** London: Frank CASS, 2005. 317 pages, end of chapter notes, bibliography, maps, index.

Few would dispute the thesis of this book: "Intelligence has been practiced in some form throughout Roman history." Even so, Professor Sheldon has assembled extensive documentation to substantiate her position. She shows how the Romans learned from experience that trust in "the inspection of the livers of sacred animals . . . [or] the consultation of oracles" (vi) were not sources

---

[18] Brig. Gen. F. J. Moberly. *Operations in Persia 1914–1919* (London: Her Majesty's Stationery Office, 1987), ii.

of reliable intelligence. In the republican period, armies gradually developed their own ad hoc methods of collection. And despite some near failures—as when Hannibal and his elephants surprised their enemies by transversing the Alps—this approach helped the Romans to win battles and build an empire. Over the centuries, as Sheldon recounts, the Roman approach to intelligence evolved from low level *exploratores* (military spies and scouts) to the more experienced *speculatores* (military couriers and clandestine agents) (165ff). She shows how these functions improved with the advent of the first state postal-messenger service, the circus publicus, and how the creation of professional informers, or *delatores*, served to protect empire officials. By 284 AD, the end of the period covered by the book, there exists the more quasi-formal "Roman secret service" or *Frumentarii* (250ff), which is eventually replaced by the dreaded *agents in rebus* (domestic security agents) (261ff). Detailed chapters cover the evolution of Roman military and domestic intelligence, although the author stresses that the Romans never had a formal, centralized intelligence organization as an institution of government. She does not make clear, however, whether that fact cost the Romans anything. In her concluding remarks, Sheldon takes up "David Kahn's law," which states, "Emphasizing the offensive tends toward neglect of intelligence" (284). Her arguments in support of this law are not persuasive. *Intelligence Activities in Ancient Rome* is a comprehensive account that demonstrates the Romans faced many of the same problems—bureaucratic and technological—that confront today's professionals. But when considering the sub-title, the reader is left wondering whether the astute Romans would have found it better to "verify" first and "trust in the gods" later.